On The Use Of The Moxa: As A Therapeutical Agent...

Dominique Jean Larrey (baron)

Nabu Public Domain Reprints:

You are holding a reproduction of an original work published before 1923 that is in the public domain in the United States of America, and possibly other countries. You may freely copy and distribute this work as no entity (individual or corporate) has a copyright on the body of the work. This book may contain prior copyright references, and library stamps (as most of these works were scanned from library copies). These have been scanned and retained as part of the historical artifact.

This book may have occasional imperfections such as missing or blurred pages, poor pictures, errant marks, etc. that were either part of the original artifact, or were introduced by the scanning process. We believe this work is culturally important, and despite the imperfections, have elected to bring it back into print as part of our continuing commitment to the preservation of printed works worldwide. We appreciate your understanding of the imperfections in the preservation process, and hope you enjoy this valuable book.

ON THE USE OF

THE

MOXA,

AS A THERAPEUTICAL AGENT.

BY

BARON D. J. LARREY,

SURGEON-IN-CHIEF TO THE HÔPITAL DE LA GARDE ROYALE, ONE OF THE OLD INSPECTORS-GENERAL IN THE SERVICE OF MILITARY HEALTH, PREMIER-SURGEON OF THE GRAND ARMY IN RUSSIA, SAXONY, AND FRANCE, DURING THE YEARS 1812, 1813, AND 1814, HONORARY MEMBER OF THE BOARD OF HEALTH FOR THE ARMY, COMMANDER OF THE ROYAL ORDER OF THE LEGION OF HONOR, &c. &c. &c.

TRANSLATED FROM THE FRENCH,

WITH NOTES, AND AN INTRODUCTION CONTAINING A HISTORY OF THE SUBSTANCE,

BY

ROBLEY DUNGLISON,

FELLOW OF THE ROYAL COLLEGE OF SURGEONS, &c. &c.

LONDON:

PRINTED FOR THOMAS AND GEORGE UNDERWOOD,
32, FLEET STREET.

1822.

Printed by T. Davis, 102, Minories.

TO

SIR WILLIAM BLIZARD, F. R. S.

PRESIDENT OF THE ROYAL COLLEGE OF SURGEONS, AND SURGEON TO THE LONDON HOSPITAL,

THE ZEALOUS PROMOTER OF MEDICAL AND CHIRURGICAL SCIENCE,

THIS WORK IS INSCRIBED,

IN TESTIMONY OF THE UNFEIGNED RESPECT ENTERTAINED FOR HIS TALENTS AND PHILANTHROPY,

BY HIS OBEDIENT AND OBLIGED SERVANT,

ROBLEY DUNGLISON.

PRESCOT STREET,
August 1st, 1822.

ERRATA.

Pag. vii. *for* AMATIUS, *read* AMATUS.

Pag. xxxvi. and xxxvii. *transpose the references to* HIPPOCRATES.

Pag. xxxvii. *for* gurgans, *read* purgans.

Pag. xlvii. *for* Ægyptioram, *read* Ægyptiorum.

Pag. 28. *for* its, *read* their.

CONTENTS.

PAG.

INTRODUCTION:

 PRELIMINARY OBSERVATIONS.—On the necessity for the payment of the greatest attention to the relation between Cause and Effect, in the study of Medicine .... i.

HISTORY OF THE MOXA .... xxvi.

 Derivation of the Term .... xxvii.

 Its present Acceptation .... xxix.

 Period of its first Introduction into Notice in Europe, &c. .... xxx.

 Antiquity of the Use of Cauterization .... xxxiii.

 Moxas of the Nomades, Indians, Persians, Armenians, Chinese, Japanese, Thessalians, Egyptians, Arracanese, Ostiaks, Laplanders, North Americans, &c. .... xxxv.

 Description of the Chinese Moxa .... xxxvii.

 Mode of preparing it .... xxxix.

 Universality of its Application .... xlii.

 Of *Acupuncturation* .... xliv.

 Mode of applying the Chinese Moxa .... xlv.

   After Treatment .... xlvi.

 Of the Egyptian, or Cotton Moxa............ xlvii.

 Moxas proposed by Baron PERCY .... xlix. & liii.

 Remarks upon the Use of the Moxa as a Therapeutical Agent.................... liv.

 Conclusion.................... lxxiv.

CONTENTS.

ON THE USE OF THE MOXA.

	PAG.
Prefatory Remarks	1
Description of the Moxa	4
Parts proper for its application	6
—— which are objectionable	7
Properties of the Moxa	8
Observations on its application	9
On Cupping	10

DISEASES FOR WHICH THE MOXA IS INDICATED:

1. Of Vision	14
Of defective action in the membranes of the globe of the eye, incipient cataract, and weakness or paralysis of the optic nerves	—
Case of Amaurosis	15
2. Of Smell	17
3. Of Taste	—
4. Of Hearing, of Voice, and of Speech	18
5. Of Paralytic Affections of the Muscular System	19
Of Tic douloureux	20
Case 1	21
—— 2	22
—— 3	23
6. Of Paralysis	24
Case of Paraplegia with Neuralgia	26
Cases of Paralysis with Neuralgia of the fore arm and hand	29
Of Hemiplegia of the Face	30
Case of	31
Of Hemiplegia of the Limbs	33

CONTENTS.

                PAG.

Case of Paralysis of the Animal Sensibility, only 34
Of Simple and Muscular Paralysis of the lower extremities 36
  Case of 37
7. Of Organic Diseases of the Head 38
  Of Epilepsy, Dropsy of the Ventricles of the Brain, Chronic Headache, &c. .... —
  Case of Epilepsy 39
  Case of Dropsy of the Ventricle of the Brain .. 41
   Ditto 43
   Ditto 44
  Of Chronic and Rheumatic Headaches 45
  Of Mental Diseases .... —
8. Of Diseases of the Chest .... —
  Of Asthma .... —
   Case of 46
  Of Intermittent Neuralgic Palpitations of the Heart 47
9. Of old Catarrhal Affections and Chronic Phlegmasiæ of the Pleura 48
10. Of Phthisis Pulmonalis 51
  Case 1 52
   — 2 53
   — 3 55
   — 4 56
   — 5 58
   — 6 61
   — 7 63
  Of Dropsy of the Pericardium and Hydrothorax —

CONTENTS.

	PAG.
11. Of Chronic and Organic Diseases of the Abdominal Viscera:	
Of the Stomach	64
Case of Disease of	65
Of Obstructions of the Liver, Spleen, &c.	66
Case of Chronic Hepatitis	67
Ditto	69
Of Chronic Congestions of the Uterus	—
12. Of Rachitis	70
13. Of Rachialgia	72
Case 1	79
—— 2	80
—— 3	81
—— 4	84
—— 5	88
—— 6	90
—— 7	91
—— 8	98
—— 9	103
14. Of Sacro-Coxalgia	108
15. Of Femoro-Coxalgia	112
Case 1	131
—— 2	135
—— 3	136
—— 4	138
—— 5	140
—— 6	142
—— 7	143
Conclusion	147

INTRODUCTION.

"Itaque non sic causa intelligi debet, ut, quod cuique antecedat, id ei causa sit, sed quod cuique efficienter antecedat; nec, quod in campum descenderim, id fuisse causæ, cur pila luderem: nec Hecubam, causam interitus fuisse Trojanis, quod Alexandrum genuerit: nec Tyndareum Agamemnoni, quod Clytæmnestram."

CICERO: *de Fato*, 15.

THE object of the Translator of the following Memoir upon Moxa, has been, to lay before the Medical Public, in an English version, the history and use of a substance, which holds an eminent rank in the therapeutics of continental practitioners: to this he has been instigated, from no English treatise, *ex professo*, being to the best of his knowledge in existence upon the subject, and from the Moxa being consequently unknown to several British practitioners, both as an object of natural and medical history. The essay, which the translator has selected for this purpose, is contained in an 8vo volume, entitled *Recueil de Memoires de Chirurgie*, by the Baron

LARREY: of which Memoirs the one upon Moxa is by far the most extended. That celebrated surgeon has been so long, and so deservedly esteemed, in this country, for the ability and zeal displayed by him, in the numerous opportunities, which he has had for pathological investigation, that, where several treatises existed upon the same subject, no explanation will be considered necessary for having preferred his memoir to that of any other writer: independently of this consideration, however, as the following treatise is a developement* of the article *Moxa,* which was consigned to the author in the *Dictionnaire des Sciences Médicales,* the translator has selected it, from its containing a more complete history of the use of the Moxa in various diseases, than any treatise at present extant.

It is but justice to observe, that highly worthy of attention as Baron LARREY may be considered, as a practical surgeon, he can never be held in great estimation as a theorist: his hypo-

---

* See Page 2.

theses being generally vague and unintelligible, and apt to spread confusion through his practical remarks:—it is, alone, as a register of cases successfully treated by the Moxa, that the work of the Baron, which is now laid before the Profession, can be considered deserving of attention.

It unfortunately too often happens, that medicines are brought forward with lofty pretensions, but which, in a short space of time, sink into that oblivion, which they frequently so justly merit: if we turn our eyes to the history of medicine, we cannot but be surprised at the immense catalogue of articles, which have been admitted into, and, in a short space of time subsequently, discharged from, the catalogue of the Materia Medica. According as the theories of the *empirical, methodical,* or *dogmatical** sect usurped the dominion of medicine, in the earliest periods of medical history, so were there remedies proposed

---

* ———Triplex quoque forma medendi,
Quæ logos aut methodos, cuique Experientia nomen.
   AUSONII *Edyll.* 11. *Lin. 67 et seq.*

to suit the prevailing theories; and amongst the moderns several have been introduced, which have been considered capable of fulfilling indications, suggested by the hypothesis which the proposer might have imbibed, from his individual notions of pathology. It is, however, to the class of *Empirici*, from the time of SERAPION of Alexandria, its founder, to the present, that we owe the introduction of several of the most important articles of the Materia Medica. By the *Empirici* of former and present days, is not to be understood the unprincipled pretender, who has his nostrum, which he gives indiscriminately in all diseases; but the man of education, who yet founds his plans of treatment, almost wholly, upon analogy, without taking into consideration philosophical induction, or the reasons which physiology might suggest to his mind, and assist him in laying down the indications of cure. The ancient *Empirics* were men of talent, and strict observation, which latter qualification they naturally acquired from their principles being founded upon the success, which they observed in analogical cases, requiring very considerable attention, in the discrimination of diseases.

The great mutability that has always been observable in medical theories and practice, however, may be fairly ascribed to a species of false experience, or want of proper knowledge respecting the laws of cause and effect: it unfortunately too frequently happens, that when a man brings forward any medicine, he is so much interested in its success, that he is often induced to view the subject through a flattering medium, and to ascribe to its action, effects to which it is not at all entitled. If we cast our eyes over the history of medicine for the last hundred and fifty years, we may see, that an almost innumerable list of medicines has been proposed, several of which have been introduced with such high recommendations in their favor, so many cases of cure obtained, according to their proposers, through their influence, that we cannot but be astonished, when we find that practitioners have subsequently excluded them from the Materia Medica. The proposer, however, of any fresh medicine, is so blinded by his prejudices, that he too generally gives a list of successful cases, not one of which perhaps owed its fortunate termination to the administration of the supposed means. Under the *Stahlian* doctrine, or what has been called by the French, *La Médecine Expectante*, and of which there are at this day several followers, we cannot but be struck with the number of cures which take place in diseases, where, from the peculiar doctrine of the practitioner, they are left principally to nature; yet had any one of the alterative remedies, which have been so extolled at different periods, been administered, the issue would have been most certainly ascribed to it, and the number of *false facts**, as Dr. Cullen would have called them, been considered sufficient to authorize a fresh addition to the already overstocked catalogue of the Materia Medica. Nothing can prove so strongly the necessity of the physical sciences forming part of the education of the medical practitioner, as the bad reasoning which is every day observable, respecting *cause* and *effect*: the study of physics necessarily habituates the mind to philosophical induction, and if a better capability of tracing effects to their causes were the

---

* *Elements of the Philosophy of the Human Mind*, by Dugald Stewart, Esq. F. R. S. Ed. vol. ii. p. 440.

only advantage to be derived from such study, it would be an acquisition of the utmost importance; independently of this, however, it is a valuable auxiliary in physiological and medical investigation: *—" Aliter enim in Physicis, aliter in foro medico tractanda est natura: illic generaliter et in communi, hic vero specialiter, ut homini est propria, respicitur."†

When AETIUS,‡ PAULUS ÆGINETA,§ and AMATIUS LUSITANUS,|| recommended *coition* as a cure for diarrhœa, and HIPPOCRATES¶ remarked

---

* *Lectures on Physiology, Zoology, and the Natural History of Man,* by W. LAWRENCE, F. R. S. Page 76,

† MICH. BERNH. VALENTIN. *Med. Nov. Antiq.* pag. 14. Francofurti ad Moenum, 1713.

‡ Tetrabib. 1. Serm. 3. cap. 3.

§ Lib. 1. cap. 35.

|| Lib. 1. Cent. 13. obs. 11.

¶ " Balbi ab alvi profluvio maximè corripiuntur longo." HIPPOCRAT. *Aphor.* 32. Sect. 6. Upon this ridiculous aphorism, the satirical SWIFT remarks, " I wish Physicians had power to remove the profusion of words in many people to the inferior parts." See SWIFT's Works, arranged by SHERIDAN, and corrected by NICHOLS, vol. x. p. 247.

that stuttering people were always subject to that affection, we cannot for a moment suppose that these observers had made remarks, which they did not consider to be authorised by their experience; yet, in all these instances, there has evidently been an accumulation of *false facts;* the connexion, between the ascribed cause and effect, being built upon no stronger foundation than in the following old, but apposite anecdote, which was related by Bishop LATIMER in the last sermon, which that prelate preached before Edward VI. :—" Here now," said he, " I remember an argument of Master More's which he bringeth in a book that he made against Bilney; and here by the way, I will tell you a merry toy. Master More was once sent in commission into Kent, to try out (if it might be) what was the cause of the Goodwin-sands, and the shelfs that stopt up Sandwich-haven. Thither cometh Master More and calleth the country before him, such as were thought to be men of experience, and men that could of likelihood best certify him of that matter concerning the stoppage of Sandwich-haven. Among others came in afore him an old man with a white head, and one that was thought to be little less than an hundred years old. When Master More saw this aged man, he thought it expedient to hear him say his mind in this matter, for being so old a man, it was likely that he knew most of any man in that presence and company. So Master More called this old aged man unto him and said, 'Father,' said he, 'tell me if ye can, what is the cause of this great arising of the sands and shelves here about this haven, the which stop it up that no ships can arrive here? Ye are the eldest man that I can espy in all this company, so that if any man can tell any cause of it, ye of likelihood can say most in it, or at least wise more than any other man here assembled?'— 'Yea, forsooth, good master, (quod this old man) for I am well nigh an hundred years old, and no man here in this company any thing near unto mine age.'—'Well then,' quod Master More, 'how say you in this matter? What think you to the cause of these shelves and flats that stop up Sandwich-haven?'—'Forsooth, Sir,' quoth he, 'I am an old man. I think that Tenterton steeple is the cause of Goodwin-sands. For I am an old man, Sir, (quod he) and I may remember the building of Tenterton steeple, and I may remember when there was no steeple at all there. And before that Tenterton steeple was in building, there was no manner of speaking of any flats or sands that stopped the haven, and therefore I think that Tenterton steeple is the cause of the destroying and decaying of Sandwich-haven."

Ridiculous as this may seem, it is an every day occurrence in medicine: in their anxiety for the success of any remedial agent, medical practitioners seem totally to forget, that the cases, which they bring forward are frequently those, which do any thing rather than prove the superior efficacy of their adopted mode of treatment. This prejudice is, unfortunately, not only confined to the *routine practitioner*, the degenerated remnant of the old *secta empirica*; but to the man of science and philosophy;[*] although it is a

---

[*] ——Homines docti (supini sane et faciles) rumores quosdam experientiæ, et quasi famas et auras ejus, ad philosophiam suam vel constituendam vel confirmandam exceperunt, atque illis nihilominus pondus legitimi testimonii attribuerunt. BACON. *Nov. Org.* Lib. 1 Aph. 98.

system, which he would highly deprecate in another. When we observe in the older writers, that DEMOCRITUS mentions that some diseases are best cured by anointing with the blood of strangers and malefactors, and others with the blood of our friends and kinsfolks; that MILETUS cured affections of the eyes with human bile; that ARTEMON treated epilepsy with dead mens' sculls, and ANTHEUS convulsions with human brains;* and when we find in the lists of the Materia Medica, such means as the *periapta medicamenta* or *amuleta*, † and still later, the *album græcum* or *canis*, the *viperæ, limaces, lumbrici terrestres, sperma ranarum, urina hominis, urina vaccæ*, the *millepedes*, and several other articles, equally absurd, admitted even into the dispensatories—we cannot but feel satisfied, that the effects, brought forward, have had no more connexion with their ascribed causes, than the

---

* PLIN. lib. 28. cap. 1.—MUFFET on *Food*, page 141.

† Amulets are still held in great repute by the Egyptians, Sumatrans, and most of the Orientals. See BELZONI's *Narrative of the operations and recent discoveries, &c. in Egypt and Nubia*, page 16.—MARSDEN's *History of Sumatra*, page 154, Lond. 1783.

building of Tenterton steeple had to do with the impeded navigation of Sandwich-haven: yet to suppose, that the learned physicians who composed the college, at the periods when several of these medicines were introduced into notice, had incorporated them into their dispensatories, without having had full opportunity, as they conceived, by experience, of judging of their powers, would be ridiculous: in proportion as the lights of science, however, have shed their influence upon us, a better knowledge as well as attention to the laws of cause and effect has been acquired, as will be evident to any one, who will take the trouble of referring to the works of the older authors on medicine or physiology. It can scarcely be credited, that the following account of the *mackerel*, as an article of dietetics, could have been written by a member of the College of Physicians, and been printed under its sanction: the treatise from which it is taken, was originally written by Dr. Muffet, who is entitled " an ever famous doctor in physick," and was afterwards " corrected and enlarged by Christopher Bennet, doctor in physick, and fellow of the Colledg of Physitians in London," and bears the imprimatur of "Francis Prujean, President, and of Balduinus Hamey, George Ent, Edmund Wilson, and Christopher Bennet, Censors."

"*Mackrels* were in old time in such request, that two gallons of their pickle (called the pickle of good fellows) was sold for a thousand pieces of silver; but time and experience described them to be of a thick, clammy and suffocating substance, offensive to the brain, head, and brest, though pleasant in taste, and acceptable to the stomach: Certain it is that they cause drousiness in the best stomacks, and apoplexies, or palsies, or lethargies, or dulness (at the least) of sense and sinews to them that be weak. *Tralianus* rightly adviseth all persons sick of fleagmatick diseases, and of stoppings, to beware of Mackrels as a most dangerous meat: albeit their liver helpeth the jaundies, being sod in vinegar, and their flesh sod in vinegar cureth the suffocation of the matrix: they are best being sod in wine-vinegar with mints, parsly, rosemary, and time, and if afterwards they be kept in pickle, made of Rhennish wine, ginger, pepper, and dill, they prove a very dainty and no unwholesome meat; they are worst of all buttered. The *French* men lay Southernwood upon a gridiron, & them upon the Southernwood, and so broil them both upon the fire, basting them well with wine and butter, and so serve them in with vinegar, pepper, and butter, as hot as can be; by which way no doubt their malignity is much lessened, and their goodness no less encreased."*

Between the time at which the work of Muffet, from which we have just quoted, was published, viz. about the middle of the seventeenth century, and a nearly corresponding period of the eighteenth, practitioners do not appear to have advanced, in their correct knowledge of the effects of medicines on the animal economy, with such rapid strides as might have been wished: on the contrary, although the doctrines of pathology were undergoing several changes, and an immense number of fresh articles

---

* See *Health's Improvement; or Rules comprising and discovering the nature, method, and manner of preparing all sorts of Food used in this Nation.* p. 157. London, 1655.

had been added to the Materia Medica, very few of which have been since retained, and several improvements taken place in the practice of medicine and surgery, yet no greater tact was acquired in discriminating the false from the true facts, as far as they related to the medicinal virtues of those articles, which act insensibly upon the human frame, and which have been commonly denominated *alteratives:* as one instance, in proof of this assertion, the elaborate account of the *viperæ*, as a therapeutical agent, in the older works on Materia Medica, an article which has been, for a considerable length of time, justly banished from our pharmacopoeias, may be adduced:*

---

* Dr. MEAD, in his *Essays on Poisons*, has the following eulogistic account of the *viperæ*.

"One of the first whom we find in antiquity to have made use of the Flesh of this Creature to Medicinal Purposes, was I think, *Antonius Musa*, the famous Physician to *Octavius Cæsar;* of whom *Pliny* tells us, *That when he met with inveterate Ulcers, he order'd the eating of* Vipers, *and by this means they were quickly healed.* It is not improbable, that he might have learn'd this from the *Greek* Physician *Craterus*, mention'd often by *Cicero*, in his Epistles to *Atticus:* who as *Porphyry* relates, *very happily cured a miserable slave, whose skin in a very strange manner fell off from his Bones, by advising him to feed upon* Vipers, *dress'd after the manner*

xvi.   PRELIMINARY OBSERVATIONS.

By several authors an appeal has been made to "long experience," in confirmation of the

---

of Fish. Be this as it will, in *Galen's* Time, the profitable qualities of the *Viper* were very commonly known, himself relating very remarkable stories of the Cures of the *Elephantiasis*, or *Lepra*, done by the Viper Wine. Aratæus, who most probably lived about the same time as *Galen*, and of all the Antients has most accurately described the *Elephantiasis*, commends, as *Craterus* did, the eating of *Vipers* as Fish, in the same Diseases. And to this purpose I remember, that as *Lopez*, in his Relations of the Kingdom of *Congo* in *Africa*, takes notice how greedily the *Negroes* eat *Adders*, roasting them, and esteeming them as the most delicious Food; so *Dampier*, also informs us, that the Natives of *Tonquin*, in the *East Indies*, do treat their Friends with *Arrack*, in which *Snakes* and *Scorpions* have been infus'd; accounting this not only a great Cordial, but also an Antidote against the Leprosy, and all other sorts of Poison.

" The Physicians in *Italy* and *France* do very commonly prescribe the Broth and Jelly of *Viper's* Flesh for much the same uses; that is, to invigorate and purify the mass of Blood exhausted with Diseases, or tainted with some vicious and obstinate Ferment."

After making these remarks, Dr. MEAD goes on to observe, " From all this it appears, that the main efficacy of the viperine flesh is to quicken the circle of the Blood, promote its due mixture, and by this means cleanse and scour the glands of those stagnating Juices, which turning to acidity, are the origin of many, at least, of those troublesome distempers, in the surface of the Body, which go under the names of scrophulous, leprous, &c." See *The Medical Works of* RICHARD MEAD, M. D. page 47, London 1762.

virtues of this article of the dispensatory—so much in use at that period,* and if such testimony be considered sufficient to prove its efficacy, in those cases which have been adduced, practitioners must, subsequently, have been guilty of great impropriety, in banishing it from the pharmacopoieas, and even, altogether, from practice; as we unquestionably are, at present, possessed of no substance of the Materia Medica, which is capable of answering all the purposes ascribed to the viperæ: the truth, however, is, that it was afterwards found, that a number of *false facts* had been accumulated in their favor; between the effects of which, and the ascribed causes, practitioners were disposed, very properly, to consider, that there was no connexion whatsoever, and it has long been the universal opinion, that they are possessed of no medicinal quality: the like may be said of the *limaces, sperma ranarum*, &c. before mentioned: the properties ascribed to them are little less ludicrous than the following directions

---

* Vide Quincy's *Pharmacopoeia officinalis*. 10th Edit. 1736.

respecting the Moxa, taken from the translation of a Japanese treatise, shewing what parts of the human body may be burnt with that substance—

"Chap. 3. Women, who would have done breeding, must have three cones burnt on the navel:

"Chap. 4. Women, that would be glad to have children, must have eleven cones burnt on the side of the twenty-first vertebra."*

Since the period (1736), at which the dispensatory of QUINCY was published, to which we have alluded, several new agents have been introduced upon the stage, which, in a short space of time afterwards, disappeared entirely from it, leaving scarcely any vestiges of their existence: of these *modi medendi*, not the least important, if we may take the noise to which they gave occasion upon their first introduction, were the

---

* See *The History of Japan*, by ENGELBERTUS KÆMPFER, M. D. translated from the High-Dutch manuscript, by J. G. SCHEUCHZER, F. R. S. Member of the Royal College of Physicians, London. 1728. Vol. ii. appendix sect. 4.

metallic tractors of PERKINS, and the inhalation of gazeous compounds, proposed by the celebrated Dr. BEDDOES; yet the use of both has been almost entirely laid aside, and we now seldom or never hear any account of them; in fact, they may be said to have fallen into almost perfect oblivion: the same may be observed of several articles of the Materia Medica:—the three kingdoms of nature have been ransacked, in order to add to our therapeutics, and scarcely one single substance has been brought forward, without some apparently strong cases of successful results being adduced, in affirmation of its efficacy: future experience, however, discovered, that the effects were rather *consecutive* than *consequent*; and their use fell into total neglect. It is this unfortunate contradiction, in the results obtained from particular means, which, more than any other circumstance, has tended to cause the practice of medicine to be considered as an almost perfectly empirical art. There are not wanting men, at the present day, who are disposed to say, and to think, that the science of medicine is not one jot better than it was in the time of

HIPPOCRATES:* this sentiment has been lately promulgated, though not in a very liberal manner, in a literary work of considerable merit, written by a learned divine,† in which he observes, that "no men despise physic so much as physicians, because no men so thoroughly understand how little it can perform: they have been tinkering the human constitution four thousand years, in order to cure about as many disorders; the result is, that mercury and brimstone are the only two specifics they have discovered:—all the fatal maladies continue to be what they were in the days of PARACELSUS, HIPPOCRATES, and GALEN—*Opprobria Medicorum*." To advance arguments for the purpose of combating the latter part of this remark, would be an idle waste of words: no man, who had paid any attention to the subject, could have thrown such a stigma upon medical science: illiberal, however, as it is, when taken as a

---

* Vide *A Treatise on Experience in Physic*, by Dr. ZIMMERMANN. Vol. i. p. 174, London 1782.

† *Lacon, or many things in few words*, by the Rev. C. C. COULTON, M. A. 1821, page 160.

whole; it is but too true, that there has always been, and still continues to be, an unaccountable vacillation or fashion in medical practice; and that but few of those agents, which have been recommended empirically, amongst which must be included almost the whole class of *alteratives*, have retained the ground, which they possessed at their first introduction; indeed, with the exception of the articles, which Mr. COULTON has mentioned, there are but very few others, which can be considered to come within an immeasurable length, of what is generally understood by the term *specifics*.

It is not to the empirical use of any remedies whatsoever, that we must ultimately look for any great improvement in the profession: by an empirical trial we, first of all, find out the sensible medical properties of any substance, and, afterwards, our physiological and pathological knowledge enables us to turn it to the greatest account; but, where the properties are by no means sensible, *i. e.* when the substance is supposed to act as an *alterative*, we should be most especially careful not to ascribe to it qualities to which it is not entitled:* it is this confusion respecting cause and effect, which (as was before observed) has tended, more than any other circumstance, to the retardation of therapeutics; for it cannot be doubted, that where the means adopted are inert, the practitioner, from a supposed opinion of their virtues, is apt to lull himself into a too fatal confidence; and, under a false security, to lose an opportunity for using more active remedies, which it is not in his power subsequently to regain. The catalogue of the Materia Medica has been undergoing a diminution, in its number of articles, for several years, and there are at present many, which, doubtless, might be very properly expunged. To physiological and pathological knowledge it is, that we must look for the most important improvements

---

* JACOBUS ROHAULT, has, in his *Tractat: Physic:* laid down three degrees of experience, which, if strictly attended to, would prevent all that confusion respecting cause and effect, which is daily observable in medicine. "Primus" he observes, "est simplicissimus sensuum usus: secundus, observationes fortuitæ sub experimentis artificialibus occurrentes: tertius, illa observatio quam ratiocinatio per varias illationes confirmat." Vide MICH. BERNH. VALENTIN. *Med. Nov. Antiq.* page 8, 1713.

in medical science;—empirical practice being perfectly subservient to it. When remedies are brought forward with too lofty pretensions, or too indiscriminately used, they frequently fall into total neglect, in consequence of their not fulfilling *all* the indications, for which the proposer recommended them, although, in several instances, their employment might be attended with the greatest benefit: of this a most remarkable case is, the use of the actual cautery;—appositely administered, it is a most useful agent, in several diseases; but, principally in consequence of its too indiscriminate adoption, it has been almost entirely banished from the therapeutics of British practitioners;—and, in the case of vaccination, there are several of its former advocates who have abandoned it, in consequence of its not fulfilling every thing, which Dr. JENNER promised on its first introduction. A more particular attention to the *series implexa causarum*, and to their relation with *effects*, will, unquestionably, remedy this false reasoning, in process of time; and, according as our acquaintance with the laws of physiology and pathology becomes more developed, medical science will be proportionably improved, and more care taken with respect to the introduction of substances into the Materia Medica, which are not worthy of a place there; or, if admitted, their effects will be more correctly traced to their causes, and, consequently, few pretensions brought forward, which they are incapable of fulfilling. It is not to credulity, but to well founded scepticism, that we are to look for those improvements in medical science, which may enable us to treat diseases philosophically, and successfully—*

" Curare appositè sanandum." CICERO.

These remarks have been suggested by some of the cases, adduced by Baron LARREY, in which the beneficial results, ascribed to the Moxa, do not appear to have owed their existence to the supposed cause; in confirmation of this, the cases detailed at p. 67, and seq. may

---

* Some interesting remarks on the general principles of Truth and Error, in the cultivation of Medicine, may be found in the *Elements of Medical Logick,* by Sir GILBERT BLANE, Bart.

be referred to, of abscesses in the liver, which broke internally, and the contents of which were discharged by the bowels: in these cases, the author ascribes the developement of the adhesive inflammation, which had commenced between the outer paries of the abscess and the intestine, to the influence of the Moxa, but without any shadow of proof—the application of the Moxa having preceded the discharge of the pus, being the only basis upon which he could have possibly founded his opinion; and, indeed, if his observation were grounded in fact, which cannot for a moment be supposed, the Moxa must be possessed of the power of acting as a counter-irritant in one case, and as a developer of inflammation in another—which seems ridiculous; the introduction of such cases would have been much better avoided, as it throws discredit upon the talents of the author for correct observation, and may have a tendency to cause those histories to be slighted, where the efficacy of the Moxa is indisputable.

The term *Moxa* has been considered, by most authors, as a word of Oriental extraction: PERCY and LAURENT, however, are of opinion, that it is to Europeans we owe the application of it to the substance, which forms the subject of this work. They observe, that the Portuguese were the first people, who called this mode of cauterization, of which they were witness, in India, China, and Japan, by the name of Moxa:—" The people of these countries," they say, " rolled or twisted small cords of certain vegetables, almost in the same manner as we prepare tobacco for smoking. Each one was provided with them, and when he wished to cauterize himself, a small piece was cut from the end of one of these cords, which was sometimes applied by the individual himself; but more commonly by regular cauterizers (*Xin Kien*), and to which he set fire, in the same manner as smokers to their tobacco, which caused the Portuguese who were witness to this operation, so novel to them, to observe, that they burnt themselves with a match, and consequently they gave the name of *Metchia, Motzchia, Moxia, Moxa, Mèche*, as well to the operation itself, as to the material which was employed for it."*

"The word Moxa," they elsewhere observe, "is not to be found in the works of the Japanese and Chinese physicians, who call it *Kieou*, and only use the term Moxa, before strangers, to whom they may wish to make themselves intelligible."

In this derivation of the word, they are not borne out by TEN RHYNE, whom they mention to have introduced it upon the continent. This latter author observes, when treating of the *artemisia*—" Hâc ergo, quæ in agris et competis provenit uberrimè, nulla frequentior planta est Japonibus, qui eam *Jomongi* et *Nophouts*, atque cum exaruerit, *Moxa* nuncupant."† It is here evidently given, as the

---

* Vide *Dictionnaire des Sciences Médicales*, article *Moxibustion*, by PERCY and LAURENT.

† Vide TEN RHYNE *de Arthritide*, page 97. The same writer, in mentioning the mode of preparing the cones of Moxa, says, " Modus eorum præparandi simplex est. Tenuiora enim folia summitatesve Artemisiæ latifoliæ (nam tenuifoliam, ut

vernacular language of the country, and there does not appear to be the least reason for believing, from any of this writer's observations, that the word is of Portuguese origin: but the evidence of KÆMPFER, who had the most ample opportunities, from a residence of a considerable duration in Japan and China, sets the matter perfectly at rest, by proving the term to be deduced from the Chinese.

" The Chinese and Japanese," he observes, " trace the origin of the Moxa to the remotest antiquity, and pretend that it was known, long before the invention of physick and surgery, and that, consequently, the use of it is sufficiently supported by a continued experience of so many ages. This ancient and so much commended caustick goes by the name of Moxa, not only in China, but in all other countries where the learned characters and language of the

---

Botanici vocant, Japonicâ, saltem quantum ego comperi, non novit) salutaris admodum plantæ, colligunt, collecta siccant in umbra (tum demum, uti supra dictum est, *Moxa* appellatur) siccata manibus fricant ambabus," &c. &c. Vide page 108.

Chinese are known, as in Japan, Corea, Quinam, the Luzon or Philippine Islands, the Island of Formosa, and the kingdoms of Tunquin and Cotsijnsina."*

When the term *Moxa* was first introduced into Europe, it was understood to signify a cone or cylinder, which the inhabitants of Japan and China were in the habit of using as a remedial agent, and which was formed of a cottony substance, procured from the beaten leaf or pith of a species of artemisia *(artemisia Chinensis)*: since that period, however, it has been used in a more general acceptation, and is now understood to signify any combustible substance, which may be employed for the cure of disease, by being placed upon any part of the body, and suffered to burn down, until cauterization is produced; but, most commonly, it is used to designate the *ustio Arabica*, or mode of cauterizing practised amongst the Arabs, and

---

* See *The History of Japan*, by ENGELBERTUS KÆMPFER, M.D. vol. ii. appendix Sect. 4. page 34.

now almost universally followed by the French practitioners.*

Whatever may have been the derivation of the term, it does not appear that the Moxa was well known, on the continent, till towards the end of the seventeenth century: about that period HERMANNUS BUSSCHOF,† TEN RHYNE,‡ and CLEYER,§ who had resided for some time in the East, returned to Europe, and published separate treatises, extolling it against many morbid affections, for which they had seen it employed amongst the Orientals.

The knowledge of this remedy appears to have reached this country, from the continental writers abovementioned, as well as from several

---

* Vide *Dictionnaire des Sciences Médicales*, article *Feu*, by M. JOURDAN.

† BUSSCHOF published his work *On the Cure of the Gout by Moxa*, in Dutch, at Amsterdam, in 1674: an English translation of which, in 8vo. was published at London in 1676.

‡ *Libro citato.*

§ ANDREAS CLEYER in *Eph: Nat: Cur;* ann. 4. obs: 1.

other treatises, which were published about the same period, in Italy, Germany, Poland, &c.* Its fame, however, upon its first introduction upon the continent, was, more especially, for relieving the paroxysms of the gout; and it appears to have been scarcely ever employed, in this country, for any other affection. Soon after BUSSCHOF had published his small treatise, upon the wonderful cures, which he had seen performed in the East, in gouty subjects, and practical confirmation of which he had experienced in his own person; Sir WILLIAM TEMPLE,† who was then at Nimeguen, and was a martyr to the gout, after having read BUSSCHOF's work,

---

* Vide PURMANNUS in *Chirurg:* P. 3. p. 292.
    PECHLINUS in *Observ:* pag. 263.
    VALENTINUS in *Polychrest: Exotic:* p. 197.
    ——— in *Hist: Moxæ cum meditat: de Podagrâ.*
    KÆMPFER in *Amœnitat: Exotic.* p. 589.
    ——— *History of Japan,* vol. ii. app. Sec. 4.
    BERN: WILH: GEILFUS *de Moxâ:* 1676.

† *Letters written by* Sir WILLIAM TEMPLE, Bart. *and other Ministers of State, &c.* published by JONATHAN SWIFT, Domestick Chaplain to his Excellency the Earl of BERKELY, &c. Page 135, vol. i. Lond. 1720.

determined upon making trial of the Moxa, when he received such considerable benefit from its application, as well as in one or two other cases in which he used it, that its fame was soon published in England: it does not appear, however, to have been much used in this country; and, in a short time, fell into such total neglect, that scarcely any writer on medicine or surgery, except in works of reference, since the time of SYDENHAM, has even noticed that such a remedy was in use for the cure of disease; and this last author refers to it, as to a subject which was by no means in general adoption by the practitioners of his time.* Of all the nations of Europe, there are none which have employed the Moxa to an equal extent with the French; although, before the middle of the last century, few individuals in France knew what the Moxa was.† POUTEAU,‡ however, about that period,

---

* *Tractat: de Podag:* page 602.

† Vide *Dictionnaire des Sciences Médicales*, art. *Moxibustion*.

‡ Vide *Mélanges de Chirurgie*, page 1, 7 & 31.
   Œuvres Posthumes, vol i. p. 202 and 626, and vol. ii. p. 36.

drew the attention of his medical countrymen so closely to the subject, by the evidence which he adduced, of the beneficial effects resulting from this mode of applying the actual cautery, in several diseases, more especially in those arising from a rheumatic or scrofulous *vice*, affecting the articulations, that this remedy began to be adopted by practitioners; since which time so many testimonials have been given in its favor, by several enlightened and observing individuals, that its fame may be said to rest on higher grounds, than that of any other remedial agent at present employed by French practitioners.

Of all the various means, which have been employed at different periods for the cure of disease, there is none which has been so universally adopted by nations, in a state of primeval simplicity,* as that of cauterizing. History

---

* In the opinion of these people, the actual fire was as useful in relieving human suffering, as Virgil describes it to be, in restoring infecund lands—

"—————— Omne per ignem
Excoquitur vitium, atque exudat inutilis humor."
            P. Virg: Mar: *Georg:* Lib. i. l. 88.

informs us that the practice was followed amongst the Aborigines of North and South America; by the natives of Japan and China, from time immemorial; by the ancient Scythians, Ægyptians, Arabs, and Laplanders; and from the testimony of several scientific travellers, who have, in modern times, attended to their medical and chirurgical practice, it appears, that the descendants of these people still follow the modes, which had been practised by their ancestors.[*]

Various are the forms which have been recommended, from the time of HIPPOCRATES downwards, for the application of the actual cautery; but we shall confine ourselves to those, which, according to the present acceptation of the term, belong to the head of *Moxa:* comprising, as was before observed, every cauterizing agent employed for the cure of disease,

---

[*] Vide BURCKHARDT's *Travels in Nubia*, pag. 340.

Histoire Générale de la Chine, Tome 13, par M. l'Abbé GROSIER.

Mémoires concernant l' Histoire, les Sciences, &c. des Chinois par les Missionnaires de Pe-Kin, Tom. 8. p. 262.

by being placed upon some part of the human body, and suffered to burn down, until it produces canterization. From the earliest ages, the Nomades employed, for this purpose, the fat wool of their flocks,* as well as certain spongy substances growing upon oaks, and springing from the hazel†—the Indian, the pith of the reed,‡ and flax, or hemp, impregnated with some combustible material§—the Persian the dung of the goat—the Armenian the agaric of the oak—the Chinese and Japanese the down of the artemisia—the Thessalian, dried moss‖— the Egyptian, Arracanese, and several oriental nations, cotton¶ — the Ostiaks** and Lap-

---

* HIPPOCRATES in *Lib. de affect.* cap. 30.

† PAULUS ÆGINETA, Lib. 6. cap. 49.

‡ KEMPFER's *History of Japan*, vol. ii. app. Sect. 4. p. 36.

§ BONTIUS *de Medicinâ Indorum*, p. 32.

‖ PERCY in *Pyrotechnie Chirurgicale Pratique*, p. 12.

¶ PROSPER ALPINUS *de Medicinâ Ægyptiorum*, L. iii. cap. 12.

** *Voyages de* M. P. S. PALLAS, Tome 4. pag. 68.

landers* the agaric of the birch — and the Aborigines of North America, rotten and dried wood, which they called *punk*.† HIPPOCRATES was in the habit of employing fungi and flax‡

---

* *Travels through Sweden, Finland, and Lapland to the North Cape,* by JOSEPH ACERBI, page 291, vol. ii.

LINNÆUS in *Lachesis Lapponica, or a Tour in Lapland,* by JAS. ED. SMITH, M. D. F. R. S. &c. vol. i. p. 274.

HARMENS and FIELSTROM, and ROSEN, *Diss. Med. Lapp. in Hall. Disput. ad Morb. Hist. Tom. 6.*

† RUSH's *Medical Inquiries and Observations,* p. 28.

‡ HIPPOC. *de affection.* cap. 8.

Since the time of HIPPOCRATES, it has been almost universally supposed that the term *Linum crudum*, signified Flax in its state of raw material. PERCY and LAURENT have, however, lately advanced an opinion, that it meant unbleached linen, and quote the following verse from Ecclesiasticus in support of their belief, " Ab eo qui utitur hyacinthus, et portat coronam, usque ad eum qui operitur *lino crudo,* furor zelus, tumultus, &c." Although the term ωμόλινον, or *Linum crudum,* might be occasionally used to signify cloth which had not been bleached; in the same manner as it was sometimes employed for a barber's cloth, which was tucked round the shoulders, whilst the hair was cutting, to prevent it from falling down the neck; yet, there can be no doubt, but that HIPPOCRATES meant by it, Tow or Flax before it had undergone any preparation, whilst the *linum coctum* signified the same substance after it had been subjected to the necessary processes for being formed into cloth: this would seem to have been the understanding which PROSPER ALPINUS put upon it; for, after having described the mode of cauterization practised by

for the same purpose, when the affected parts were situated near the bone; and so great was his opinion of the actual cautery, in the cure of disease, that he considered it, under any of its forms, as the *dernière ressource*, the remedy *par excellence*. " Quamcunque partem dolor occupaverit, balneis, fomentis, linimentis emollire, et alvum subducere, levato dolore gurgans exhibere, post hæc lac asininum potare, &c. si in unum aliquem locum irruerit dolor, et constiterit nec medicamentis expellatur, inurito, quocumque in loco fuerit."*

The Chinese Moxas are formed from the

---

the Egyptians, by means of the cylinder of cotton, surrounded by linen cloth, which will be hereafter mentioned, observes, " Non tamen modum inurendi, qualem Ægyptii frequentant, ullum antiquorum vel juniorum medicorum cognovisse comperi, nisi dixeris Auctorem Lib: de affectio: tali experientiâ aliquando usum fuisse, cum ad coxendicum dolorem et ad podagram, inustionem lino crudo faciendam tradiderit. At isti non *lino crudo*, sed *cocto*, atque gossipio, id præsidii genus exercent." Vide PROSPER ALPINUS, Lib. 3. cap. 12.

Vide also upon the same subject, FABRICIUS ab Aquapendente, *de Operationibus Chirurgicis*, cap. 93. 106.

CELSUS, *de Ani Fistulis*.

* HIPPOC, *de internis affect*. cap. 53.

dried leaves of the *Artemisia vulgaris latifolia*, or *Artemisia Chinensis:** the leaves are plucked off when the plant is very young and tender, and are hung out in the open air for a considerable time. The Japanese consider, that it is not, at all times, equally proper to gather the artemisia for this purpose; but that it must be done only on those days, which have been selected by their astrologers, and which are thought to possess the advantage of a particularly benign influence of the heavens and stars, by which the virtues of the plant are greatly increased: these are the first five days in the fifth Japanese month, called by the natives—*Gonguatzgonitz*, which, according to the Gregorian calendar, answers to the beginning of June, and sometimes, but seldom, to the latter end of May; the Japanese commencing their year, with the new moon next to the spring equinox. The plant is gathered early in the morning, before it loses

---

* FURSTENAU, *in Observ. de Indor. Morb.* 15.
Moxa made from the *Artemisia vulgaris* in Germany, was found to answer very well. See *Eph. nat. Cur.* Dec. 3. A. 7. 8. app. 141.

the dew; it is then hung in the open air, on the west side of the house, until perfectly dry, and afterwards laid up in the garret: the older it is, the tenderer and better down may be obtained from it, for which reason it is sometimes kept so long as ten years. The fresh artemisia receives the different names of *Tuts, Nophouts, Jamoggi* or *Jomongi*, according to its different stages of growth, and of *Moxa* when dried; this change of names, according to circumstances, is not confined to plants, but is also applied to other things, according to their different uses; as well as to men when they come of age, or are advanced to any considerable post.*

The preparation of the Moxa, is a matter of no great art or difficulty, although it was formerly kept a great secret by the Chinese, being sold in their shops, ready prepared, only.†

---

* Vide KÆMPFER's *History of Japan*, vol. ii. App. Sect. 4. TEN RHYNE *de Arthritide*, pag. 108.

† Vide *Miscel. Cur. Med. Phys. Acad. Nat. Cur.* ann. 1675—6, obser. 224, JOHANNIS SIGISMUNDI ELSHOLTII *de Moxâ*.

The leaves are, in the first place, beaten with a pestle, or rubbed between the hands, until the coarser fibres, and harder membranous parts, are separated; the *tomentum*, or down, which remains, is then kept for use: this, when formed into small cones or pyramids, of about the size of a pea each, is the most common mode of making the Moxa, amongst the Chinese, as well as the Japanese.* Sometimes, they fold the purified down of the herb in paper, and roll it with the palm of the hand, until it is equably and compactly put together; from which, with a knife, they cut off small pieces, of about the thickness of two quills *(duos circiter scriptorios calamos crassas)*, which they place upon the pained part, and, after having set fire to, suffer to burn down.† M. LARREY observes that M. KLAPROTH, the younger, after the return of the latter from China, presented to him a Moxa, of the form and size of an ordinary crayon *(un crayon ordinaire à dessiner)*, which he used with

---

* TEN RHYNE, *libro citato.*

† *Ibid*, pag. 109.

the greatest advantage, in every case, where he could not apply the cotton cylinder. These small Moxas were composed of powdered phosphorescent wood, and lycopodium, and were, according to M. LARREY, easy of imitation.*

The most common caustic in use amongst the Brahmins, or Gymnosophistæ of the ancient Greek writers, and the Indian heathens, is the pith of the junci, or rushes, which grow in morassy places: it is not material what sort of rush it is, provided it is somewhat thicker and larger than the common scirpus. This pith they dip into the oil of the seed of the sesamus, and burn the skin after the common manner.†

According to KÆMPFER, the Chinese and Japanese burn indifferently, and without regard, old and young, rich and poor, male and female:

---

* *Mémoires de Chirurgie Militaire et Campagnes*, du Baron D. J. LARREY, vol. iv. page 407.

† KÆMPFER's *History of Japan*, vol. ii. App. sec. 4, p. 36.

‡ *Ibid*, p. 39.

women big with child are alone spared, if they have not been burnt before. The intent of burning with the Moxa, is either to prevent or to cure diseases, but it is more particularly recommended, by their physicians, as a preventive medicine, for which reason they prescribe it to the healthy, more frequently than to the sick: this practice they ground upon the principle, that by the very same virtue by which it dispels and cures present distempers, it must, of necessity, destroy the seeds of those to come; and, by that means, prevent them. Hence it is that, in those extremities of the East, all persons who have any regard for their health, cause themselves to be burnt, once every six months. This custom is so thoroughly and so religiously observed, in Japan, that even those unhappy persons, who are condemned to perpetual imprisonment, are not deprived of this benefit, but are taken out of their dungeons, once in six months, in order to be burnt with the Moxa*. The neighbouring black nations make more use of the Moxa than

---

* TEN RHYNE, *libro citato*.

the Chinese and Japanese themselves, in epilepsy, and all chronic disorders of the head: their plan is, to burn a considerable quantity of it along the sutura coronalis, which has been sometimes attended with so much success, that some patients are said to have recovered, who had been previously given over by their physicians.*

In all the northern provinces of China, the principal remedy, for most diseases, consists in making deep punctures in the body, upon which small balls of the down of the artemisia are burnt: these punctures are made with needles of gold, silver, or steel, without drawing blood; and all the skill required in the physician, is to determine their number and depth, and where it is necessary to make them:† this plan is famed, not only for curing, but for preventing several diseases, especially the gout and rheu-

---

* KÆMPFER, *libro citato*.

† *Histoire Générale de la Chine*, par M. l'Abbé GROSIER, tom. 13.

matism, the former of which is said to be unknown in China.* It was formerly considered that every kind of fire was not proper for lighting these salutary balls, and, therefore, mirrors of ice or metal were employed for that purpose: they caused the water to freeze in a round convex vessel, and the ice, being presented to the sun, collected its rays, and set fire to the down of the plant.† The practitioners, who apply the Moxa, are called, by the Chinese, *Tensasi*.‡ TEN RHYNE observes, that *acupuncturation*§ has become a peculiar art, in Japan,

---

* *Travels in China*, by JOHN BARROW, F. R. S. p. 354.

† *Description Générale de la Chine*, par l'Abbé GROSIER, tom. ii. p. 549.
Mémoires concernant les Chinois, tom. v. p. 517.
Narrative of a Journey in the interior of China, &c. by CLARKE ABEL, M. D. F. R. S. F. L. S. &c. Page 218.

‡ KÆMPFER, *libro citato*.

§ Within the last few years, *Acupuncturation* has been employed upon the Continent, as well as in this country, and apparently, with considerable success: but few trials, have, however, been made of it.
See *Dictionnaire des Sciences Médicales*, art. *Acupuncture*. —*Mémoire sur les Maladies Chroniques, les évacuations sanguines et l'acupuncture*, par L. V. J. BERLIOZ, D. M. Paris, 1816.

and that those who perform it are called *Farritatte (id est Acupunctores)*, but if they join with it the application of the Moxa, as many do, they are called, in Japan, *Farrawyts tensas*, and, in China, *Xinkieu*: their houses are known by the wooden image of a man being placed in the vestibule, on which the places for acupuncturation and the application of the Moxa are delineated.*

In applying the Moxa, the base of the cone or pyramid is placed upon the part, intended to be burnt, and the top set fire to by means of an aromatic *bacillum*, called by the Japanese *senki*, and which is similar to those, which the heathen priests burn in their temples; they burn slowly, are of a strong, fragrant scent, and are made from the powdered slimy bark of the *taab* tree, as they call it, or *taabnoki*, (the Laurus Japonica sylvestris, or wild Japanese bay

---

A Treatise on Acupuncturation, &c. by JAMES MORSS CHURCHILL, Member of the Royal College of Surgeons in London.

* TEN RHYNE *de Arthritide*, pag. 189.

tree,) made into an electuary, with aloes wood, and other sweet scented spices, and afterwards formed into *troches* or *bacilli*.*

After the Moxa is burnt down, bruised garlic is applied to the eschar†, and if a blister is produced by this substance, it is opened with a pair of scissors; but the eschar is suffered to separate by nature: to assist this, a heated plantain leaf *(folium plantaginis tostum)* is applied, so that the rough back is turned to the eschar; but if it be the intention to heal it, without giving rise to suppuration, the soft side of the leaf is put to the part: in want of the plantain, a cabbage leaf, and in default of that, the emplastrum diapalma, or basilicum, is sometimes applied; indeed, this last application is made use of, along with the plaintain or cabbage leaf, for the purpose of retaining it in its situation.‡

---

* KÆMPFER, *libro citato*.

† TEN RHYNE, *libro citato*.

‡ Vide *Miscell. Cur. Med. Phys. Acad. Nat. Cur.* Ann. 1675 and 1676. Obs. 224, JOHANNIS SIGISMUNDI ELSHOLTII, *de Moxâ Sinensi antipodag*.

The mode of preparing the Moxa, most generally, however, adopted, in the present day, on the continent, is, according to the Arabic or Egyptian manner, or what has been called the *ustio Arabica*—the form of cauterization practised by the wandering Arabs and Egyptians: of this Baron LARREY has given a description in the following pages,* which, it will be observed, bears a very close analogy to the following account of the Egyptian Moxa, given by PROSPER ALPINUS,†—" Volentes inurere aliquam partem corporis, sumunt lineam petiam, cubiti longitudine, latitudineque trium digitorum, atque gossipii justam quantitatem, quod totum linea prædicta petia involuunt, ac filo serico ligant ad formam pyramidis, ipsiusque latiorem extremitatem urendæ parti applicant, probèque cuti adhærere student, alteramque caput vel extremum succendunt, comburique permittunt, quousque fasciculus ille ex linea petia, atque gossipio omnino crematus sit, continuè dum cutis uritur, carnem circum circa ferro tangentes,

---

* See page 4 and seq.

† *De Medicinâ Ægyptiorum*, cap. 12.

ne ex eo calore aboriatur interea aliqua inflammatio; observant etiam dum involucrum illud parant ut in ejus medium sit foramen vel meatus, per quem fiat aliqua respiratio atque eventatio." This, with very little alteration, is the plan which POUTEAU, who has the credit of having revived the use of the Moxa, in Europe, adopted,* and which has been followed, with but few modifications, by nearly all the practitioners since his time. The Arabians, and those Asiatic nations who received their arts and sciences from them, as, for instance, the Persians, and those of the Great Mogul's subjects who embraced the Mahometan faith, are said never to make use of any other caustic than woollen cloth, dyed with *glastum* or woad. The caustics of the Arabian physicians are made of a substance, dyed with a decoction of this plant, from a supposition that it increases the efficacy of the fire, which supposition they declare to be far from imaginary, but to be grounded upon a continued experience of many centuries. This

---

* *Mélanges de Chirurgie.*
Œuvres Posthumes, tom. 1 & 2.

opinion of the Arabians, is supported by a notion, which prevails very much amongst the common people, in some parts of Europe, that burning a piece of cloth, dyed blue with woad, and holding it under the nose of a person in an epileptic fit, will remove the paroxysm more effectually, than the smoke of white linen, or of any other stuff whatsoever.*

In consequence of the inconvenience which Baron PERCY found to attend the application of the common cotton Moxas, from the necessity of employing the blow-pipe, until the whole of the cylinder was consumed; he was induced to substitute Moxas formed of some combustible material, impregnated with nitre: this idea he confesses to have acquired from the following quotation from FABRICIUS ab Aquapendente: †
" Per linum crudum, uti supra CELSI testimonio dictum est, cap. de ani fistulis, puto HIPPOCR.

---

* KEMPFER's *History of Japan*, vol. ii. app. sec. 4. p. 36.

† Article *Moxibustion* in the *Dictionnaire des Sciences Médicales*.

intelligere linum ignitum; atque uno verbo dicam, chordam factam ex lino crudo intorso, ut est chorda sclopeti, quæ ignita servat ignem, nisi quod sclopeti chorda cocta est, quæ vero ab HIPPOCR. usurpabatur erat chorda non cocta."*

In this sentence, it will be observed, the author does not give us any reason for supposing, that he had ever himself employed the *gun match* or *chorda sclopeti*, as a Moxa: PERCY, however, in his *Pyrotechnie Chirurgicale*, † published towards the end of the last century, gave to FABRICIUS the credit of having made use of it for that purpose; this error he subsequently corrected;‡ but, at the same time, committed another, by ascribing to himself the originality of the employment of the *match:* if he had referred to BONTIUS, who published his work *de Medicina Indorum*, about the commencement

---

* *De Operationibus Chirurgicis*, cap. 106.

† *Pyrotechnie Chirurgicale Pratique*, p. 77. Paris, Edit. 1811.

‡ *Dictionnaire des Sciences Médicales*, article *Moxibustion*.

of the seventeenth century, and who lived, consequently, nearly about the time of FABRICIUS ab Aquapendente, he would have found that BONTIUS has remarked, that the Orientals were formerly in the habit of applying the *chorda sclopeti* as a cautery:—" Cucurbitæ quoque affigantur cervici, scapulis, ac vertice raso capiti, incolæ arterias crotaphis seu temporales, laminâ candente, vel *fune sclopetario* accenso, urunt, cum stupendo fructu, quod etiam faciunt in omnibus capitis longis doloribus.*

According to PERCY,† they have no other Moxas in the French army, than those cut from the gun matches, which are sometimes applied in the state of chord, and, at others, after having been reduced to a lanuginous form: he recommends that flax, hemp, or any porous and soft vegetable substance, should be put into a strong solution of nitre; which solution must be afterwards evaporated, until the flax, hemp, or other

---

* BONTIUS *de Medicinâ Indorum*, p. 32. Paris, 1645.

† Article *Moxibustion*.

substance, is left dry: when it may be kept for use: but, the Moxa which he extols above all others, is the *meditullium* of the *helianthus annuus*, or great sunflower, which "Nature" he observes, "has impregnated with the nitrate of potass, which causes other Moxas to burn so well." He directs the stalks to be well dried in the sun, to be cut into pieces, half an inch long, and kept free from mould and moisture. "The bark of the plant," he says, "left in the form of a ferule, round the pith, serves as an envelope to the Moxa, which may, by this means, be managed as we like, and held with the fingers so long a time as is necessary, without risk of their being burnt:—so slow is this species of envelope in being heated!" Another advantage which he considers this "*medullary Moxa*" to possess, is, that the pain of the burning may be diminished, during its application, by pressing upon the cortical covering, and by burying, a little, in the skin, the end which is applied to it.*

---

* Article *Moxibustion.*

Notwithstanding the recommendation of Baron PERCY, that the Moxas should be formed of flax, hemp, cotton, or other substance, impregnated with nitre; the plan has been but rarely made use of, in France, more especially, in consequence of the cauterization being more sudden, more severe, and in every respect more similar to the action of the metallic cautery than the Moxa in ordinary use, described by Baron LARREY;[*] ", Every thing," says M. ROUX, "'should tend, that the combustible substance which we employ may consume slowly, and without interruption, so that the heat be prolonged, and insensibly carried to its greatest intensity: it is upon this that the efficacy of the remedy depends."[†] This object would not be answered by those substances which are strongly impregnated with nitre, more particularly if the intention of the physician were, like M. LARREY's, merely to produce a superficial burn: the *meditullium* of

---

[*] Page 4—and page xlvii. of this Introduction.

[†] *Dictionnaire des Sciences Médicales,* article *Feu,* by M. JOURDAN.

the *helianthus annuus*, however, appears to possess every advantage which a Moxa can have; and independently of the convenience of being so easily attainable, it is, according to PERCY, unattended with the inconveniences, which he has conceived to accompany the application of the cotton Moxas, as usually formed.

In concluding the History of the Moxa, it may not be improper to make a few observations upon the qualifications which it possesses as a therapeutical agent: and, if we give full credence to the cases, detailed in the following Essay, as well as to the works of the authors to whom reference has been made, it must be allowed, that those qualifications are by no means despicable; on the contrary, there can be no question but that the Moxa is an agent, of the greatest efficacy, in the cure of several diseases.*

---

* " This *heroic* remedy, which has several times been the subject of my clinical Lectures at the Hôpital de la Garde, has particularly fixed the attention of the foreign physicians, who constantly attend these lectures, and notwithstanding the little

The high encomiums that have been passed upon it—the apparently strong cases which have been adduced of its efficacy, and its frequent use amongst continental practitioners, several of whom are men of the greatest science, entitle it to considerable attention from British practitioners: according to those authors, it may fairly be said, in the words of a celebrated lawyer and statesman, upon another occasion:—" Si antiquitatem spectes est vetustissima, si dignitatem est honoratissima, si jurisdictionem est capacissima:" for several reasons, however, it has never been sufficiently attended to, by practitioners in this country, whilst, on the continent, it has, on the contrary, like most other favorite remedies, been applied too indiscriminately.

---

confidence which they at first possessed, respecting the efficacy of this remedy, they yielded to evidence, and, at present, not only eulogize, but have generally adopted it, as the most advantageous means, in the treatment of some chronic affections, reputed incurable; such as the Disease of POTT (vertebral disease), that of the Coxo-femoral Articulation, Phthisis Pulmonalis, Scirrhus of the Pylorus, &c." See the preface to the *Recueil de Mémoires de Chirurgie*, by BARON LARREY.

An unfounded idea has been hitherto entertained by most medical practitioners in this country, who have not taken sufficient pains to inform themselves to the contrary, that the Moxa is never employed but as a caustic issue, and that its efficacy is merely dependant upon the discharge produced by it: this opinion has been promulgated in standard works of reference,* in which, the inconveniences, attending the application, have been carefully detailed, and even magnified, whilst its reputed good effects have been slightly passed over.

One of the most common of the objections that have been adduced against it, is the great degree of pain which it occasions, but even this has been greatly exaggerated; to say that its application is not attended with pain would be ridiculous, but it is by no means of that superlative degree which has been mentioned; and moreover, were it so violent as has been described, provided it be an agent of such

---

* Cooper's *Surgical Dictionary*, art. *Moxa*.

considerable efficacy, as there is every reason for believing it, from the strong examples which have been brought forward in its favor, the objection, as in cases of the most severe surgical operations, would fall to the ground, since it would seldom be employed, except in diseases which had resisted other means, and which, in all probability, either would prove fatal, or be productive, if left to themselves, of considerable subsequent distress and misery:

" Ad extremos morbos, extrema remedia exquisitè optima." *

Those gentlemen, however, who have seen its application on the continent, must have noticed, and even been somewhat astonished, from their previous prepossessions to the contrary, at the comparatively trifling expressions of pain, which have escaped patients, whilst undergoing this operation. Medical practitioners, since the time of Dionis and Sharp more particularly, have imbibed so great an abhorrence of the actual cautery, under any of its forms, that it has been

---

* Hippocrat. *Aphorism.* 6. sect. 1.

frequently laid aside, in consequence of such prejudice, in cases, where its application might, probably, have been attended with considerable benefit; and there can be but little doubt, that the Moxa has been neglected, in this country, in consequence of its being considered as productive of all the pain and inconvenience attending the actual cautery, when used in a metallic state: this idea is, however, by no means correct; the light, porous substances of which the Moxa is fabricated, during their combustion, are frequently productive of a degree of heat so trifling, as merely to produce rubefaction, and irritation of the cutis vera, without even occasioning suppuration: indeed, in the following pages, it will be observed, that M. LARREY frequently applies the Chinese Moxas[*] upon the face, and, he particularly observes, that they occasion little or no deformity, the suppuration

---

[*] M. LARREY does not confine the term *Chinese Moxa*, to the Moxa, formed according to the manner of the Chinese and Japanese, detailed in a former part of this Introduction, but uses it to signify the common Cotton Moxa, made much smaller. See the wood engraving at page 4.

being prevented, by the prompt application of the liquor ammoniæ,* and the eschars falling off in the form of thin scales, from the tenth to the thirteenth day.

Sir WILLIAM TEMPLE, VAN SWIETEN, and POUTEAU, who applied the Moxa to their own bodies, have given a description of the sensations they experienced, during the cauterization, which by no means equals the degree of suffering, which has been supposed to be occasioned by it: and although POUTEAU may be justly supposed to have been somewhat prejudiced in favor of the cotton Moxa, from his anxiety to have the substance introduced into France, it cannot be imagined that the other two, whom we have mentioned, were guided by any other desire, than that of giving a correct history of the effects produced by the Moxa, under the belief, that it would be the means of diminishing, if adopted in practice, the afflictions of suffering humanity. In *An Essay upon the Cure of the*

---

* See pag. 30 and 33.

Gout by Moxa, written to M. de Zulichem, and dated, Nimeguen, June 18, 1677,* Sir William Temple thus describes his sensations, during the application of the Moxa:—" For the pain of the burning itself, the first time it is sharp, so that a man may be allowed to complain: I resolved I would not, but that I would count to a certain number, as the best measure how long it lasted: I told six score and four, as fast as I could, and, when the fire of the Moxa was out, all pain of burning was over. The second time was not near so sharp as the first, and the third a great deal less than the second. The wound was not raw as I expected, but looked only scorched and black; and I had rather endure the whole trouble of the operation, than half a quarter of an hour's pain, in the degree I felt it the first whole night." The testimony of Van Swieten,† is, in every respect,

---

* *Letters written* by Sir William Temple, Bart. *and other Ministers of State, &c.* Published by Jonathan Swift, Domestick Chaplain to his Excellency the Earl of Berkely, &c. Page 135, vol. i. Lond. 1720.

† Gerardi L. B. Van Swieten *Commentaria* in Hermanni Boerhaave *Aphorismos.* Tom. 4. pag. 385.

similar—" Applicui proprio femori longe majorem Moxæ conum, et facile tolerare potui illum dolorem. Gliscit enim sensim ignis per artemisiæ lanuginem, sicque gradætim augetur calor, donec sensim auctus tolerabilem satis ustionis sensum faciat." The quotations, which have been given, relate to the Chinese Moxa,* which, in consequence of being so much smaller than the Egyptian, is, of course, attended with a minor degree of pain. Of the sensation experienced during the application of this latter, Pouteau gives the following account †—" I, at first, felt the part warmed by an agreeable heat, but which soon became unpleasant: it would have even become insupportable, had its violence been of longer duration: I knew, however, by

---

* " The Pain is not very considerable, and falls far short of that which is occasioned by other caustics or actual cauteries."

" I have seen many times the very boys suffer themselves to be burnt in several parts of their body, without shewing the least sense of pain." Kæmpfer's *History of Japan*, vol. ii. app. sec. 4. page 39.

See also *Narrative of a Journey in the Interior of China, &c.* by Clarke Abel, M. D. F. R. S. &c. &c. page 217.

† *Mélanges de Chirurgie*, page 49.

the trials which I had made, that the pain was most violent when the fire destroyed the papillæ of the skin, and that it became less afterwards, although the heat continued to extend more deeply into the body of the skin. It was nearly a quarter of an hour, before the cauterization was finished; all which still proves that it is not so cruel, as one might, at first, have imagined, by the pain, which a superficial burn of the finger occasions."

Another most important objection to the employment of the Moxa, were it founded on fact, is, that even in those cases where its success may have been manifest, similar results might probably have been obtained from a " caustic issue, a blister, or volatile liniments:"* this is, however, a mere *gratis dictum*, and we may thus, if inclined to be sceptical, doubt the greater efficacy of any remedy whatsoever, and choose to observe, that another, less severe in its operation, might have, perhaps, answered the

---

* Vide *A Dictionary of Practical Surgery*, by SAMUEL COOPER, art. *Moxa*.

purpose equally well: on a reference to the history of medicine, we may find, that the same objection has been made to the first introduction of several most important improvements in therapeutics, by which, many valuable lives have, unquestionably, been preserved.* The observations of British practitioners can have no weight, however, upon this subject; for the Moxa, most assuredly, has never had even the shadow of a fair trial in this country: some few cases have occurred, where it has been employed, but they have been so rare, and so imperfectly followed up, that no negative or affirmative respecting its good effects can be deduced from them.† As

---

* Neither DIONIS nor SHARP, who expressed in such strong terms their dislike of the Actual Cautery, could exceed GLANDORP in his *Tirade* against Caustics: he observes; " Ego verò ut verum fatear in totâ praxi meâ à septici usu abhorrui, illudque cane pejus et angue fugi, et tanquam zizaniam relegavi, rejecique." *Gazophylacium,* cap. 7.
Œuvres Posthumes de POUTEAU, tom. i. page 271.

† Vide *An Essay on Neuralgia of the Inferior Maxillary Nerve,* "*Nervus Mandibulo-labialis,*" *cured by operation, by* Mr. JOHN LIZARS, in *Edin. Med. and Surg. Journal,* Oct. 1821.

In the preface to the *Recueil de Mémoires de Chirurgie,* BARON LARREY observes, that he had received a letter from

was before observed, it has been, with us, the common practice to consider the action of the Moxa to be, in every respect, similar to that of a caustic issue; but this is by no means the principle upon which it is applied by several of the continental practitioners: indeed, so little do they depend upon the discharge occasioned by it, that, in several cases, detailed in the present work, as well as in those of several writers upon the same subject, the suppuration has been prevented, or when it may have taken place, has not been encouraged: the principal advantage, which is ascribed to it, is, its acting as a powerful counter-irritant: there may, indeed, be instances, where the good effects of the remedy may be still further increased by the establishment of suppuration, but these

---

Dr. GRANVILLE, requesting some Moxas, similar to those which he had seen M. LARREY use at his Hospital, accompanied with a description of the manner of making and applying them; Dr. GRANVILLE, at the same time, stated, that from the success which Baron LARREY experienced from their employment, he should endeavour to introduce them into use, as they were unknown in this country.—From the known talents of this author, we look forward with an agreeable anticipation to some communication, respecting the results which he has experienced from the employment of the Moxa. See Pref. p. viii.

consecutive effects are generally considered of secondary importance: now, if in those cases, where caustic issues are thought to be indicated, equally beneficial results are likely to be obtained, from the counter-irritant properties of the Moxa; the latter means would, certainly, be attended with less inconvenience than the former, and might, perhaps, in other respects, produce less injury to the general system: moreover, the pain, attending the Moxa, is only of very short duration, whilst that attending caustics is considerably prolonged.*

---

* It was the opinion of the celebrated Mr. POTT, that the utility of caustics in the vertebral disease, was entirely owing to the quantity of matter, which they discharged, checking in some manner the caries, and giving nature an opportunity of exerting her powers of throwing off the diseased parts, and producing by incarnation an union of the bones, (rendered sound) and thereby establishing a cure; and that it was of very little importance towards the cure, by what means the discharge was procured, provided it was large, came from a sufficient depth, and was continued for a sufficient length of time. Mr. POTT also remarks, that he had tried the different means of setons, issues by incision, and issues by caustic, and that he had found the last in general preferable, most cleanly, most easily manageable, and capable of being longest continued;* Baron LARREY, on the contrary, considers, that the

* Vide POTT's Works, vol. iii. page 455.

HISTORY OF THE MOXA.

When M. Roux, one of the surgeons of La Charité, was in London, he had two opportunities of applying the Moxa, and although neither was completely successful, partly owing, perhaps, to his not having had an opportunity of following up the application, so frequently as was necessary, yet it seems, in both instances, to have produced an almost immediate benefit: the case of white swelling, which he had an opportunity of treating at Guy's Hospital, we shall give in a version from the author's own words, and, it will be observed, that the opinion of M. Roux tends to confirm, what was before mentioned, respecting the exaggerated statements, which have been made, of the pain, occasioned by this cauterization.*
" Mr. Cooper," he says, " desired me to apply it, under his own eyes, upon a young woman, who felt the pain, very violently, on the outside of the patella: it was upon this part that I burnt a tolerably large cotton cylinder: the pain diminished so considerably, and so speedily, in

---

* See *Rélation d'un Voyage fait à Londres en 1814, ou Parallèle de la Chirurgie Angloise avec la Chirurgie Françoise*, p. 20 et seq.

the part, where the Moxa was applied, that, some days afterwards, the patient expressed to Mr. COOPER, in my presence, that she would willingly support other applications of the Moxa, if they were judged to be necessary for her cure; she even appeared desirous, that another should be quickly applied, upon the internal side of the articulation. In this young woman, the disease was too far advanced, to give any well founded hopes of a favorable termination: in all probability, it will have since continued to make progress, but in a more slow and indolent manner: and, more especially, it will have been accompanied with more supportable pain. I informed him, from what experience had taught me, that such would be the only results, from the application of the Moxa, in this case, but I announced them as nearly certain. If the event has justified my prediction, the English surgeon will, without doubt, have less repugnance, for the future, in making use of the Moxa, and I may perhaps have done something towards naturalizing, among them, this means, so *heroic*, and so powerful in many cases. May I observe, *en passant*, that the application of the Moxa is not so cruel, but that we see many persons bear it, for the first time, without giving signs of very acute pain; and others, who have appeared to suffer more, but who have had but little aversion to having it repeated a considerable number of times."

Finally—in the preface to the work, whence the Essay upon Moxa, the translation of which forms the substance of the present work, was taken, Baron LARREY has made the following additional remarks, respecting the employment of that agent: " The publication, in 1812, of three volumes of my *Campagnes*, the first of which contains a plate, representing the instruments for the Moxa, had already aroused the attention of practitioners to this curative means: since that period, the memoir, accompanied with plates, inserted in the fourth volume of the same work, published in January, 1817, as well as the article *Moxa*, in the *Dictionnaire des Sciences Médicales*, (tom. xxxiv.) have extended its employment over all Europe, and I have, for a long time, had the satisfaction of learning, that several foreign physicians have obtained unlooked-for success from it. It is to be desired, that in France, they would have less repugnance to make use of this cautery, unquestionably much less cruel than that of POTT, the pain of which, though less acute, is much more distressing, from its being so long continued. The effects of the Moxa are, moreover, much more advantageous, as I consider I have demonstrated; and, although the cautery of POTT is still preferred by several celebrated surgeons, I have every reason for hoping, that the cases detailed in these opuscula, and the experience of physicians, who actually make use of the Moxa, will convince every mind, and dissipate the prejudices, which still exist against this cauterization. Since the printing of this memoir, I have collected a considerable number of facts, which confirm, more and more, the truth of my assertions.* I have not entered into any long *exposé* of the diseases, for which I have

---

* " One of my colleagues will make known, in considerable detail, the case of a Grenadier *à cheval* of the guard, named LEMAIRE. This young man, had been under treatment in my wards, in consequence of a slight wound, for a Phthisis

employed the Moxa, with success. Desirous to confine myself, as much as possible, to the sense of the title of this *Recueil*, I have considered that I might leave to physicians the faculty of explaining, at greater length, the effects of the topical remedy, which I extol: but, I may observe upon this occasion, that there are very few severe diseases, which can be treated with any certainty of success, without the aid of surgery, which I may call, with Marcus Aurelius Severinus, Lapeyronie, and many other celebrated authors, *effective medicine (La Médecine efficace).*

From a comparison, then, of the testimonies, which have been adduced by various celebrated continental surgeons, regarding the efficacy of

---

Pulmonalis in its third stage: from twenty-five to thirty Moxas, and a mild regimen, conducted him to a perfect cure, so that he has regained his former *embonpoint.*

Dr. Chardel, a distinguished physician in the metropolis, will, doubtless, also publish the history of an extremely violent case of Tic douloureux of the face, for which every kind of treatment had been vainly employed. Thirty-five Moxas caused the disease to disappear, and Madame de Ch***, the subject of this case, was restored to perfect health."

the Moxa, with the *altera pars*, or objections, which have been brought against it, the man of science will be enabled to decide, whether it appears to be possessed of sufficient virtues to induce him to make use of it in practice. In a country, blest with so many excellent institutions for the relief of disease, opportunities are incessantly occurring, where the medical officers might put it to the test of experience, and if it should be found to possess the whole, or, even, but half, of the powers, which have been ascribed to it, it will be much more worthy of a place amongst our therapeutical agents, than many, which have, from time to time, been admitted.

British practitioners have imbibed such a horror of the actual cautery, under any form, that some difficulty may be found in taking an impartial view of its effects;—even in questions of chemical science, where, it might, *à priori*, be imagined that no difference could arise between the experiments instituted, the greatest discrepancy is sometimes observable; the results being differently given, according to the previous bias of the parties: how much more likely, then, are we to expect discordance, where the relation, between cause and effect, is so difficult to be traced, as in medicine:—when such strong testimony, however, has been given, as in the case of the Moxa, by several enlightened Foreign practitioners, who cannot be supposed to be interested in its success, from any other desire than that of alleviating human suffering, it behoves the scientific individual to pay every attention to the observations, which have been brought forward, and not to decide respecting it, until after a full and fair trial, endeavouring to lay aside any prejudices, which he may have previously imbibed, although a task, by no means free from difficulty, for—

"Dediscit animus sero, quod didicit diu."

With respect to the execution of the following essay, the translator would merely observe, that he has, as much as the different idioms would permit, adhered closely to the author's words;—

"—— Verbum verbo reddere fidus,
Interpres."

and, where obscurity has occurred, he has,

occasionally, added notes, by way of illustration: with respect to the author's theories, however, which are frequently vague, and, sometimes, almost perfectly unintelligible, he has passed them over without comment, and the reader may, perhaps, be disposed to do the same. The British practitioner, who has been taught to despise the doctrine, may be inclined to quarrel with the retention of the humoral pathology; a doctrine, which the author maintains, in common with his medical countrymen: but the translator, considered that he could not have performed his duty faithfully, had he substituted any other terms, for those of the author: besides, the man of science, in his zeal for prevailing systems, and his antipathy to those, which may have been exploded, should consider, that although the humoral pathology may be fundamentally erroneous, the difference frequently consists, only, in phraseology; and that some of our most prevalent ideas are precisely those of the humoral pathologist, but under different terms—thus, a *sanguineous defluxion*, upon any part, is synonimous with a *determination of blood*; and the employment of a blister, as a *derivative*, as expressive, as to say, that it acts as a *counter-irritant*.

The whole of the work the Translator submits, diffidently, and respectfully, to his medical brethren, and should it have the effect of drawing their attention seriously to the subject, and of informing gentlemen, who might otherwise have been unacquainted with it, respecting the history of an agent, which is so much, and, frequently, so usefully employed by continental practitioners, he will consider that he has not written in vain.

ON THE USE OF

MOXA.

During my campaigns in North America, Egypt, and Syria, having had an opportunity of confirming the observations of authors and travellers, respecting the great advantages which the people of those countries derive from the use of Moxa, in several morbid affections; I availed myself of every occasion which occurred in my practice for making trial of it.

In the first place, I took into consideration the nature of the diseases which appeared to me to require its use, and afterwards, observed attentively the effects of this Cautery in its mode of action, whether as applied after the manner of the ancients, (generally adopted) or after the modifications which I have caused it to undergo: I have even followed, in the dead body, the traces of the impressions which this Cautery had left, when, (its action being rendered insufficient, owing to the too advanced state of the disease) it had not been able to re-establish entirely, the equilibrium of life.

The happy and extraordinary results, which I have generally obtained from its application, in a great number of desperate cases, have induced me to develope in this memoir, the article which is appropriated to the Moxa, in the *Dictionnaire des Sciences Medicales;* where there is, moreover, but a small account of it: and I consider that this new work will not be without its use, either to the public who are imbued with an unfortunate prejudice against this remedy, or to those physicians who are partisans of " expectant medicine,* *(la médecine expectante)* and who have not had an opportunity of practising in large hospitals.

The people of Asia and Africa have, very justly, passed the highest encomiums upon the Moxa, not only for the removal of many diseases, which had resisted the use of other means, but also for preventing them, and for preserving health; and this sovereign remedy would certainly have enjoyed its reputation, so justly merited, more generally, amongst European nations, if, like the Chinese or Egyptians, it had been applied with proper precautions: by return-

---

* " *La Médecine Expectante*" is used to signify that plan of treatment, in which, diseases are suffered to proceed according to their natural course, without being opposed by vigorous means.
Tr.

ing to the simplicity and perfection of its first mode of application, we have been enabled to procure from this agent all the advantages which the ancients ascribed to it, and to remove the inconveniences, which had, with equal truth, been attributed to it, when the application was not made with the proper degree of judgment.

In the description which I am about to give of this Cautery, I shall endeavour to draw the reader's attention to its efficacy under every possible circumstance; neither shall I dwell upon its origin, which appears to be lost in the obscurity of time; nor upon its various forms, nor manner of application, according to the people who may have made use of it.—Very circumstantial details on these subjects may be found in the Dictionary already quoted, by the celebrated PERCY, under the word Moxibustion*

I shall, in the first place, give a description of the Moxa, as we employ it. I shall afterwards point out its mode of application, the regions and particular points of the human body upon which it may be placed, and in order to give a just idea, I have subjoined a plate containing the back and front views of a doll, with the places

---

* See also the Translator's Introduction to this Work. *Tr.*

proper for the application of the Moxa marked upon it.* I shall afterwards make known the specific properties of the Moxa, and its general effects at the time of its application. The diseases for which I have employed it with success, shall be then succinctly traced, analyzing as much as possible its particular effects in each of them. And finally, I shall detail cases relating to it, which I have collected in the course of a practice of more than thirty years; after which, I am persuaded no one can be longer doubtful of the great advantage, which art may derive from this cautery, if more generally used.

The cone or cylinder of Moxa is composed of a certain quantity of cotton wool, over which, a piece of fine linen is rolled, and fastened at the side by a few stitches,—as represented in the margin.† This conical cylinder should be about an inch long, and of a proportionate thickness: the size, however, may be varied according to circumstances.

---

* These figures are executed in such a careless manner in the original work, as well as in the *Dictionnaire des Sciences Medicales*, that no correct idea can be obtained from them; they have therefore been omitted, and more especially as the verbal description which follows, points out the author's meaning in a manner sufficiently intelligible. *Tr.*

† The upper figure represents a Chinese Moxa, and the lower, one of cotton enveloped in fine linen.

DESCRIPTION OF THE MOXA. 5

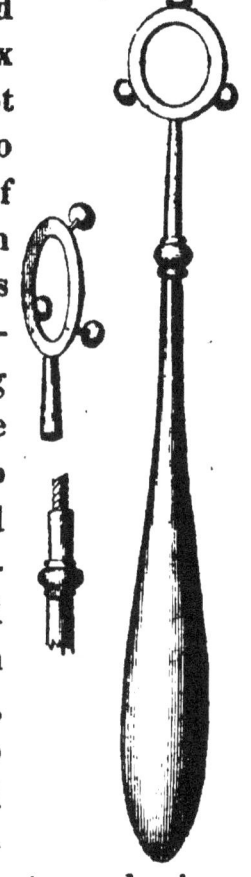

A Porte-Moxa, also represented in the margin, is intended to fix this cylinder upon the precise spot where we wish the application to be made. The metallic ring of this instrument is isolated from the skin, by three small supports of ebony, which is a bad conductor of caloric. After having set fire to the extremity of the cone, the combustion is kept up by means of a blow-pipe; it should not, however, be too much hastened, on the contrary, it should be made to go on slowly. In order to apply the Moxa properly, the precise spot, where we wish to place it, should be first marked with a little ink, and all the surrounding region covered with a wet rag, having a hole in the middle, so as to leave bare the part which has been marked: this rag prevents any sparks from coming in contact with the skin. After having set fire to the top of the Moxa, the base of it, held in the Porte-Moxa, must be placed upon the intended part, and, by means of the blow-pipe, the combustion be kept up until the whole is consumed. In order to prevent the great inflammation and abundant suppuration, which would be the consequence, the liquor ammoniæ should be immediately applied to the burnt part; this may be done even by dropping it from the bottle.

According to authors, the Moxa may be placed upon all parts of the body. I agree, however with some of them, that there ought to be excepted;

1st. All that portion of the cranium which is only covered by the skin and pericranium; there the effects of the Moxa, and *a fortiori*, those of the Actual Cautery, act too immediately upon the membranes of the brain, as well as upon the brain itself: whence fatal events may result, of which a great many instances have occurred.*

---

* See *Œuvres Posthumes de Pouteau.* vol. ii. page 44.

Author.

Since the time of POUTEAU, and notwithstanding the cases which have been detailed by that author, as well as by DEHAEN, of what they considered fatal results, from the application of this cautery to the head; it has been strongly recommended and generally adopted by Baron PERCY, VALENTIN, GONDRET, and others; not only under the form of Moxa, but also under that of the Metallic Actual Cautery. In several cases of affections of the brain, not only have the integuments been destroyed by the application, but the soft parts have in repeated instances been divided, and the actual cautery placed upon the denuded bone, so as to occasion an exfoliation of the external table of the skull: our astonishment is not so much excited by

DEHAEN relates two cases which confirm the danger of the application upon these parts.

2dly. Neither should it be applied upon the eyelids, the nose, nor the ears: we should equally avoid its application over the course of the larynx, the trachea, the sternum, the glandular parts of the breast, the linea alba, and the parts of generation; unless it be upon the perineum, towards the origin of the canal of the urethra, for schirrous and chronic enlargements of these parts, particularly of the prostate.

3dly. We should abstain from the application of every kind of cautery, over the course of the superficial tendons, and over those parts of the joints, where we should have any fear of injuring the articular capsules.

---

the cures, which are related to have taken place from this severe operation, as by the few instances, which are upon record of serious injury occasioned by it. The interdiction of the application of the Moxa also upon several other parts, appears to be somewhat problematical. PERCY is of opinion, that it may be applied upon every part of the body, except the face, excluding this region in consequence of the considerable deformity likely to be occasioned by it; but even this part it will be observed has been subjected by the author to the action of the Moxa, without being attended with the inconvenience mentioned by PERCY; so that it would appear there are but few regions of the body, which have not been laid under contribution, for the application of this cautery. *Tr.*

The properties of the Moxa are different from those of the Metallic Actual Cautery, the effects of which latter appear to be confined to the part touched by the fire: this part is disorganized to a greater or less extent, according to the bulk of the cautery, and the degree of its application. It is accompanied with a severe, sharp pain, which is borne with difficulty, and sometimes it is followed by the destruction of the subcutaneous nerves, and by a very abundant suppuration; whilst the Moxa, which is burnt slowly, is less terrific, and the pains more progressive. It has, moreover, appeared to me to communicate to the parts, along with a corresponding mass of caloric, a very active volatile principle which cottony substances furnish, when they are in a state of combustion. The irritation and excitation resulting from the combination of these two products, which are developed by the insufflation, are gradually propagated to the most deepseated parts, so as to restore the action of the weakened or paralyzed nerves, and to stop the progress of the morbid cause, seated in any particular part. When we wish to produce merely superficial effects by the Moxa, it may be permitted to burn down without making use of the blow-pipe.—This is the plan of my honorable colleague, Baron Percy.

I shall endeavour to explain the excitant effects

of the Moxa, when speaking of the causes of the diseases, for which it appears to me to be indicated. During its application, I have remarked that the first degree of heat produces a sensation, rather agreeable than painful; but pain soon succeeds, and increases progressively, until it is at last, unquestionably, very severe: the patient, however, supports it the more courageously, because he is prepared for it, and knows, by experience, after one application, that it is almost immediately removed by the prompt application of ammonia.

The number of the Moxas must be varied according to the nature and duration of the disease: one or two may be applied at a time, but an interval of several days should be left between each application, because the intrinsic effects of one or two Moxas, at the most, are equal to those of a greater number, applied at the same time, and upon the same part; but, besides that the latter would be unnecessary, they would be attended with the double inconvenience, of producing a degree of pain which the patient could not support, and of causing (from the number of the burns,) a too abundant suppuration, which might be followed by hectic fever: for these reasons, then, it is better that they should be applied by one or two at a time. Moist weather is less conducive to the success of this application, than dry and serene, which latter should consequently be preferred. In order to assist the beneficial effects of this remedy, in many cases, cupping, either dry, *mouchetées*,* or *scarifiées*, should be premised, and its use should be followed by the internal exhibition of remedies, appropriate to each disease. As cupping is a powerful auxiliary of the Moxa, and as its revulsive properties are very analogous to those of this cautery, before going farther, I shall enter into a short digression upon that subject.

A cupping vessel is made of glass or other transparent substance, such as horn, of a pyramidal or bell shape, intended for the purpose of producing a vacuum upon any part of the body, where it may be applied, by means of an exhausting syringe, which is fitted to it, or of some combustible substance, which is set fire to, in its interior, at the moment of its application; the intention, in cupping, being to produce a certain revulsion from the internal affected parts towards the external, with or without loss of blood, according to the indications to be answered. In order to fulfil this intention with all possible success, the vacuum under the cupping glass should be produced by means of some combustible

---

* See page 13.

substance, which may rarefy or abstract the air contained in it, by producing such a quantity of caloric, as, when applied to the skin, may penetrate through it, without, however, occasioning burning, so that the capillary vessels of this envelope, after having been distended by the expansion of the aeriform fluids which they contain, and being no longer compressed by the external air, in consequence of its having been abstracted or considerably rarefied, are slightly inflamed by the contact of the caloric, caused by the combustion of the substance made use of for this purpose, and thus an artificial erysipelas is produced: but the most simple, most prompt, and least painful mode of procedure, and the one which produces this result the most easily, is, to burn a little fine tow in a common cupping glass, so that the combustion may take place at the bottom of the vessel. The mass of caloric, and the action of the cupping glass may be increased, by dropping upon the tow a small quantity of any alcoholic liquor, but this is more especially necessary when dry cupping is made use of.

Cupping, by means of the exhausting syringe, is not attended with the same advantages; for, besides the inconvenience arising from its heaviness, as well as from the necessity of having so many glasses, furnished with copper screws, for the purpose of being adapted to the exhausting syringe, it has that of abstracting the local heat, along with the atmospheric air, and of producing a degree of cold in the part where the vacuum is made: and, in fact, the temperature is there very sensibly diminished. A simple tumefaction, therefore, is alone produced, in that part of the skin which is inclosed by the cupping glass, without the least redness; so that the derivation caused by it is not worth mentioning; we have therefore need of scarifications, or of punctures, more or less deep, in order to obtain a sufficient quantity of blood; and this kind of solution of continuity is not without its inconvenience: sometimes small filaments of subcutaneous nerves are wounded, which gives rise to nervous affections; and sometimes small arteries, producing hemorrhages difficult to arrest, of which I have seen many examples. This objection applies equally to every instrument with a spring, and which cannot be managed at will, whilst the scarificator which I use, and which I invented,* makes punctures as superficial or as deep as may be required. These punctures, moreover, embrace all the surface of the skin, which is rubified by the cupping glass, and are made with nearly as much promptitude as those produced by the catch of the English or German

---

* It is a species of modified fleam. *Author.*

scarificator,* with the difference, that those made with our scarificator, are less painful and more uniform. In short, experience has proved to us that our mode of cupping is the best and the most convenient: along with the Moxa, it contributes considerably to the cure of diseases, for which this latter remedy is indicated; and it is more especially proper in every species of phlegmasia; leeches not being at all comparable with it.

I shall proceed to point out succinctly, and as

---

* This comparison between the French and the English mode of Cupping, appears to be very hypothetical, notwithstanding what the author has observed, respecting the confirmation which experience has given of the greater advantages of the French method. Baron LARREY is evidently much biassed in favor of his own invention, for he has totally overlooked the circumstance of the English Scarificator's being provided with a screw, by which the depth of the punctures made by the instrument, may be regulated at pleasure. The author has, in the following pages, frequently alluded to two modes of cupping,—*Les Ventouses Mouchetées*, and—*Les Ventouses Scarifiées*, which he appears to use almost indiscriminately, and, even when he prefers the one to the other, he does not state his reasons for so doing. Both the *generic* terms have been retained in this English translation, the former of which,—*Mouchetées*, the author has adopted when the punctures were made superficially, either with the point or shoulder of a lancet, or with the instrument of his invention; whilst the latter,—*Scarifiées*, he has used when the punctures were made more deeply by the same means. *Tr.*

methodically as I possibly can, the diseases for which the Moxa is indicated; and to make known the modifications which should be adopted in its application, in each of them; beginning with the disorders of the sensitive organs, and proceeding, successively, to the enumeration of all those, where this cautery is employed with advantage.

1.

OF VISION.

Defective action in the membranes of the globe of the eye, incipient cataract, and weakness, or recent paralysis of the optic nerves, indicate the application of the Moxa, which should be placed upon the course of the nerves most connected with those of the eye, such as the trunk, and principal ramifications of the facial, those of the superior maxillary, and of the frontal. The excitation communicated to these nervous branches, spreads progressively, and arrives by degrees at those affected with the morbid principle; the effects of which are gradually dissipated, and the vital properties of the diseased organs re-established in the same proportion.

To the excitant property of the Moxa, which is the most efficacious, we may join, if it be desired, the revulsive and derivative effect, which the suppuration from the cauterization by the Moxa produces, when it is suffered to take place: the cases where this last mode is necessary, are easily distinguishable from those where it is useless, and sometimes, even injurious. By this remedy I have arrested, most particularly, the progress of Amaurosis or Gutta serena, and, in some cases, have caused it to disappear, where the blindness had been complete. Many instances may be found in the history of my campaigns, but that of the little Englishman, detailed in the third volume of those memoirs, being one of the most remarkable, I shall relate the particulars of it.

This blindness, according to the father's account, had suddenly come upon him, when crossing the Asturias, during the severe cold of the winter to which they had just been exposed. This cold had, necessarily, a much more injurious effect upon him, from his having had his hair recently cut close, and from having travelled from Corunna to Valladolid, barefoot. There could be no doubt of the existence of amaurosis in this child: the iris of each eye, however, preserved its movements. It would be difficult to describe the situation of the father, a corporal in the British army, and the great affliction, into which the unfortunate state of his son had thrown him. As the blindness was recent, I had great hopes of curing the little patient, who was, besides, very interesting. After having put him, with his father, in the best ward of the hospital, and having had him well washed, in a bath of soap and water, he was put upon the use of diaphoretic bitters, and the Moxa was applied over the course of the facial nerve, behind the angle of the jaw, and a camphor liniment was rubbed over the head, which I took care to have immediately covered with a woollen cap. At the second application of the Moxa, the child saw the light; at the fourth, he already distinguished objects and colours; and, finally, after the seventh, the sight was completely restored.

When along with the paralytic affection of these parts of the eye, which we have just pointed out, there are joined symptoms of plethora, in the vessels of the affected parts, the application of the Moxa should be preceded by that of cupping, *mouchetées* or *scarifiées*, on the temples, the nape of the neck, or the shoulders; and, if necessary, bloodletting from the jugular vein, or from the temporal artery, should be had recourse to. Leeches, without being attended with the advantages of cupping, have the inconvenience, especially when applied near the eye, of producing an ecchymosis, which increases the internal asthenia, and the turgescence in the conjunctiva.

The number of the Moxas, must be relative to the duration and intensity of the disease; and the effects of this efficacious remedy, may be aided by aromatic, discutient fumigations, dry or moist, directed upon the eyes; by weak embrocations of camphorated spirit upon the eye lids; by the internal use of colomel, alone, or in combination with other substances, according to the nature of the case; and by electric sparks given off to the upper eye lid, where the Moxa cannot be applied, should it be paralyzed.

2.
OF SMELL.

I have obtained no success from the application of the Moxa in some individuals who had lost their sense of smell. It appears that the peculiar modifications which the olfactory nerves undergo, in the pituitary membrane, for the purpose of receiving the impression of smells, render the nervous tissue of that membrane, inaccessible to the stimulating effects of the Moxa, so that I consider this remedy useless in such affection.

3.
OF TASTE.

The same may be said of the taste. Experience having taught me, that the Moxa, has no effect upon this sense.

4.

OF HEARING, OF VOICE, AND OF SPEECH.

When deafness is occasioned by the impression of a sedative and stupifying cause, such as cold applied suddenly to the ear, or by the influence of a keen and moist air upon this part, the Moxa, which is infinitely superior to blistering, applied over the course of the nervous branches of the facial, and around the meatus auditorius, restores the hearing; the excitation, produced by the heat of this cautery, being the more easily communicated to the auditory nerve, from its intimate anastomoses with the little sympathetic. I might relate a great many examples of cure, obtained by the Moxa in cases of deafness, produced in the manner I have supposed; but I shall confine myself to a succinct account of some of them.

A young trumpeter in the cavalry of the guard, after having imprudently bathed in the Seine when in a state of great perspiration, was suddenly struck with loss of voice, and inability of hearing the loudest sounds. The nature of these infirmities, was at first mistaken, and they were treated as feigned. The patient was however removed to the hospital of Gros Caillou, in order to be put under my care. After having cupped him *(mouchetées)* several times upon the nape of the neck, as well as between the shoulders, a series of Moxas was placed over the course of the principal branches of the nerves, which I have mentioned: at the third application, the young patient began to hear loud sounds, and to articulate some words; at the seventh and ninth, the articulation was almost perfect, and the hearing very considerably improved: finally, after the thirteenth Moxa, this trumpeter was sent back to his regiment, completely cured. I have obtained similar success in other young persons, whose cases are related in my *Campagnes*,[*] and in whom the deafness and dumbness supervened, from causes analogous to those which produced them in this trumpeter.

5.

OF PARALYTIC AFFECTIONS OF THE MUSCULAR SYSTEM.

I shall now proceed to notice the effects of the Moxa on paralytic affections of the

---

[*] *Memoires de Chirurgie Militaire et Campagnes.* Tr.

locomotive system, with or without neuralgia,* beginning with the first mentioned.

When the convulsive and habitual movements of certain muscles (which characterizes the tic douloureux) have become chronic, whatever may have been their cause, or are the result of some mechanical agent, which has weakened the nervous tissue of its muscles, the Moxa is completely indicated: but it should be applied as near as possible to the seat of the disease, and over the course of the injured nerves. This injury consists in a chronic and inflammatory turgescence *(engorgement)* in the *néurilème*,†

---

* The term *Neuralgie*, is used by the French writers, to signify any irritation attacking a nervous trunk; the principal effects of which are an extremely acute, lancinating pain, following the ramifications of the nerve, and commonly returning by paroxysms. MONFALCON is of opinion that neuralgia only differs from rheumatism, phlegmon, or phlegmasiæ of the mucous or serous membranes, by the nature of the tissue which is affected, and that if nerves are susceptible of inflammation, (which he considers it would be a " Medical Heresy" to doubt), then neuralgiæ are their inflammations. This it will be observed is also the opinion of Baron LARREY.   *Tr.*

† This term is used by the author, as well as by REIL, BICHAT, and others, to signify the sheath, membrane, or canal which surrounds the medullary portion of the nerve; and which two united, according to universal acceptation, form the *nerve* itself.   *Tr.*

which envelopes the nerves of the part affected. This remedy communicates an excitation to these organs, produces a salutary derivation of the morbid principle which alters their tissue, and re-establishes the course of the nervous fluid. The Moxa would not be equally indicated in acute neuralgiæ proceeding from spontaneous causes, or in tetanic affections, because it increases the irritation, as well as the tetanus: in the latter case I have employed it, but without any success. I shall proceed to detail some cases, which leave no doubt respecting the success of the Moxa in the chronic tic douloureux, a disease which almost all physicians consider incurable.

A young soldier, of the ex-imperial guard, laboring under a tic douloureux of the left side of the face, was sent to the military hospital of Gros Caillou, in 1811, six months after having received a blow, with a fencing foil, on the cheek bone of the same side, and over the course of the infra-orbitar nerve. This disease had withstood the application of leeches, alkaline liniments, and blisters, which had been applied to the temple, and behind the ear of the same side. Six Moxas placed over the course of the infra-orbitar nerve, and the corresponding branches of the facial, entirely removed the involuntary, convulsive, and almost habitual contractions, which he had experienced in the affected part.

Madame D*** had been afflicted for many years, with a tic douloureux, which began in front of the right ear, and extended in diverging rays, following the direction of the branches of the temporal nerve, towards the top of the head, the forehead, and to the eyelids of the corresponding eye. The attacks were periodical, but very violent; they were followed by headache, sudden palpitations of the heart, oppression, with spasm and icy coldness of the extremities. The convulsive contractions of the muscles of the eyelids, occasioned a complete occlusion of the eye, and prevented the patient from seeing even the light on that side, during the paroxysm.—A great number of remedies, more or less recommended, had been ineffectually tried in the country as well as in Paris.

After having seen this lady in one of these paroxysms, I examined attentively the affected parts, and made myself acquainted with every thing, which could throw any light upon the causes and progress of the disease. The principal temporal branches of the facial nerve, were easily felt by the finger, in the form and of the firmness of small violin strings, and the gentlest pressure, made upon them, caused the most acute pain. This neuralgia being complicated with derangement of the greatest part of the organs of internal life, I first of all fulfilled the indications, which such derangement presented to me, and when I considered that the chief disorder was isolated, I applied the Moxa. Three small cylinders were successively placed over the course of the trunk, and the principal branches of the facial nerve, and six Chinese Moxas* upon the branches or cords above mentioned.

Each application was followed by a sensible amelioration, and every nervous symptom had entirely disappeared before the ninth.

This lady returned, completely cured, to her usual place of residence, in one of the northern departments, where she now enjoys perfect health.

A second lady, of a more advanced age, Madame de B***, had been affected for many years with a tic douloureux, of all the left side of the face, along with an incipient hemiplegia *(un commencement d'hémiplégie)* of the same side, the symptoms of which shewed themselves

---

* Vide Introduction. *Tr.*

most particularly during the paroxysms of the neuralgia.

A great number of remedies had been tried, but without effect. With this lady, as with the first, before the application of the Moxa, I prescribed cupping, *(mouchetées)* and other means which were indicated. She likewise underwent a treatment adapted for combatting the morbid cause of the neuralgia, which I should not have been able to cure permanently, without such means.* This was continued for a considerable length of time after the Moxas, the number of which, great and small, was carried to eleven. To my great and agreeable surprise, this lady now enjoys perfect health: her disease was one of the most severe, that I have ever witnessed.

6.
OF PARALYSIS.

Paralysis, properly so called, has many de-

---

* The author has here, as well as in several other instances, very much diminished the interest of his cases, by not entering sufficiently into detail. It is impossible to say what the treatment to which he alludes could have been:—in all probability, however, (as the author considers Neuralgiæ to be depending upon an inflammatory state of the nervous tissue) it consisted of antiphlogistics, combined with the means which he has mentioned. *Tr.*

grees, and a relative duration: it is sometimes confined to asthenia of the locomotive powers, without the animal sensibility being at all injured by it: in some very rare cases, this latter faculty is entirely destroyed, whilst the contractile power of the muscles remains untouched; or else, these two properties are affected at the same time, which constitutes complete Paralysis. We also very often observe, that the paralytic affection of the muscles is accompanied with an increase of the animal sensibility, which is manifested by pain, and by preternatural and involuntary movements of the affected limbs.

In cases of the first description, the morbid principle has appeared to me, to bear its effects upon the substance even, of those portions of the encephalon, in which the nerves of locomotion, or of the animal sensibility, have their origin; or, upon the tissue of the nerves themselves. This nervous substance, when once attacked by the morbific principle, after having undergone changes, relative to the stages of the disease, finally becomes wasted, and entirely loses its vital properties. In the examinations, which I have made, of the bodies of those who have died, laboring under Paralyses of long standing, I have found the nerves of the affected side much smaller than those of the sound limb, and of a dull colour, with the character of atrophy.

The latter affection having some affinity to the tic douloureux, I shall begin by relating the success, which I have obtained by the Moxa, in that disease. Here, I had thought to have remarked, that with the derangement in the nervous substance, there is joined a sort of phlegmasia of the *néurilème* of the nerves, or of the cerebral or spinal membranes, which, along with the asthenia in the movements, gives rise to a degree of neuralgia. The Moxa is a no less efficacious remedy in this case: it acts in two ways: viz. by communicating an excitation to the weakened tissue of the portion of the spinal marrow, or of the affected nerves, sufficient for the restoration of the nervous fluid; and by the suppuration which accompanies the burns of the Moxa, and which produces a revulsion of the phlegmasia. This suppuration is not necessary in the case of a simple Paralysis, unaccompanied with neuralgia; but, in the first instance, we should allow the burns from the Moxa to suppurate, and, commonly, it is indispensably necessary, prior to its application, to prescribe cupping, *(mouchetées)* over the course of the injured parts, according to my method.

M. P. counsellor in Paris, had been afflicted for three years, along with exhaustion of strength, by a paraplegia with neuralgia, characterized by a total loss of the power of sustentation, and of progression;—by severe and almost permanent pains, with shaking and emaciation of the lower limbs;—by want of sleep, and extreme irascibility. All the remedies indicated in such cases, had been ineffectually tried. The nux vomica, of which they had been desirous to make trial, had increased the neuralgia, without at all augmenting the tone of the muscles.* After having made use of cupping, several times, at proper intervals, upon the lumbar region, and over the course of the principal nerves of the lower extremities; I began the application of the Moxa, by two at a time, commencing at that part of the spine, where the disease appeared to have its origin: this was at the tenth and eleventh dorsal vertebræ; the spinous processes of which, jutted out preternaturally, and upon which pressure by the finger caused great pain. The first application relieved the pains; which gave encouragement to the patient: the two next were immediately followed by spontaneous movements

---

* The trials which I have made of this remedy upon some paralytics, have had a similar result; it cannot be doubted, that, far from dissipating the phlegmasia of the nervous membranes, it augments it. I have remarked, that its effects are constantly pernicious, and I think, contrary to the opinion of some physicians who extol this medicine, that it is one of those which should be expunged from the Materia Medica.

Author.

in the limbs, and by such a delightful calm, that, for the first time since a long period, he enjoyed a perfect and uninterrupted sleep, for the space of eight hours. After the eighth Moxa, he was able to hold himself upright, and to proceed a few steps, with the aid of crutches. The pain, and shaking of the limbs, had entirely disappeared by the tenth application, and the contractile power of the muscles was sensibly increased. Each subsequent application augmented the strength and action of all the vital properties of the limbs; so that its nutrition was, in the same degree, restored. This amelioration went on gradually, under the influence of the Moxas, which I applied by two at a time, at relative distances, but never at a less interval, than of five or six days. They were suffered to suppurate slightly, for the reasons which I have before assigned. When we had reached the twenty-sixth Moxa, he was able to go to the theatre, on foot, with a single support. At the thirty-second, I considered that his cure was as complete as possible, and, what is very surprising, M. P*** is able to walk for a very long time, with the aid of a stick, without pain or faltering. He no longer feels pain in his limbs, which have nearly recovered their primitive shape and size.

In this paraplegic, a phenomenon, in some respects singular, presented itself, and which I have not seen in such a sensible manner in other paralytics similarly treated; viz. that each application caused contractions in the feet and legs, as strong as those occasioned by galvanism, when applied to the denuded nerves of these limbs: an experiment which I was the first to perform upon limbs recently amputated.*

On my return from Belgium, in 1815, I found, at the Military Hospital of Gros Caillou, two soldiers of the Imperial Guard, affected with paralysis and neuralgia of the forearm and hand, produced by a gun-shot wound of the arm. In the one, the projectile had traversed the limb in its lower third, passing behind the os humeri; and in the other, it had traversed the middle part of the arm in front of that bone. In these two subjects the paralysis was confined to the muscular action, whilst the animal sensibility was elevated. One of them, especially, felt the most violent pain, in his hand and fingers, accompanied with a sort of unpleasant tingling at his fingers' ends. Emollients and narcotics, particularly opium, had been ineffectually tried. The paralysis and pain had gone on increasing, and they begged for amputation, as the only means for putting an end to their torments. I

---

* See the *Bulletin de la Société Philomatique*, Mar. et Juin. 1793, tom. i.   *Author.*

encouraged them as much as possible, and took them under my care. After having washed the limbs with strong soap and water, the Moxa was applied above the cicatrices, and over the course of the injured nerves; proceeding from above, downwards: the pain and tingling quickly disappeared, and the motion was gradually restored in all the muscles of the fore arm and hand. One of the soldiers left the hospital perfectly cured, some months afterwards. The second, who had been sent to the Hospital of Val-de-Grâce, in order to be cured of an itchy eruption, *(d'une Eruption Psorique)* which had supervened, during the treatment of his wound, was attended in this latter hospital by one of my old pupils, M. DESROUELLES, who continued the application of the Moxas, from which similar success was obtained.

The hemiplegia of the face has hitherto been considered, by authors, as incurable; because they durst not apply the Moxa upon the face; and in truth, when this substance is employed after the usual method, it produces extensive and deep ulcerations, the effects of which are sometimes more distressing than the disease itself: on this account, these same authors have been induced to prohibit its application upon this part; but the modifications which I have adopted, have enabled me to use the Moxa, as well upon the face, as upon other parts of the body; only, I have taken care to make the cotton cylinders smaller, and to prevent the suppuration of the burnt parts by the application of ammonia.

The first subjects, attacked with this kind of hemiplegia, and cured by these means, were young soldiers of the imperial guard, who, in consequence of the wet bivouacs of the first campaign in Prussia and in Poland, had one side of the face paralyzed. The eye of the side affected, remained open during sleep, and the corner of the mouth, on the opposite side, was drawn up, by the contraction of the muscles which remained sound, &c.

The repeated application of small Moxas over the course of the branches of the facial nerve, and upon some of the anterior branches of the cervical, restored the action of the paralyzed muscles.

The cases of these young soldiers are inscribed in the registers of the Hôpital des Gardes: I shall dispense with relating them here, and confine myself to that of a young person, whom I had an opportunity of treating in town, with similar success; the disease presented the same symptoms, but it was owing to a different cause. Mademoiselle de M***, since become Madame D***, about seventeen years of age, of a nervous and very delicate constitution, possessing, along with the graces of the mind, the highest accomplishments, had been afflicted from her infancy, with a hemiplegia of the left side of the face, supervening a worm fever.

Electricity, and mineral waters pumped upon the part, had been employed, but without effect: the deformity was extreme, and gave to this young lady, (otherwise very pretty,) a disagreeable look, especially when she suffered the least smile to escape her.

The desire of being freed from this horrible deformity, induced her to undergo, contrary to the opinions of several physicians, the application of the Moxa, which I had proposed to her, as the only remedy likely to be efficacious. I had a small Porte-Moxa, made on purpose, and I applied the first cones, over the course of the trunk of the facial nerve, at its exit from the foramen stylo-mastoideum: thence I followed, in three diverging lines, the direction of the principal branches of this nerve; making the application at relative distances. They were unquestionably painful, but the young patient, at all times very courageous, bore them without uttering a single cry. The prompt application of the fluid volatile alkali, immediately took away the pain: the eschars from the Moxa dried up, and fell off in little black scales, from the tenth to the thirteenth day; they left a very small reddish cicatrix, which time and washing with soap and water entirely effaced. At the fourth application, there was an evident change in the disease; the improvement, however, proceeded but slowly, until the ninth; afterwards, it was progressive, and after the seventeenth, the cure was completed; the two commissures of the lips were parallel, and the articulation, which, before the treatment, had been very defective, was become perfect. The occlusion of the paralyzed eye, was not entirely effected; but with the exception of this deformity, the muscular actions of the face, were almost entirely re-established.

Hemiplegia of the limbs, especially when it has become chronic, is much more obstinate, and unless recent, it is difficult of cure; because the portions of the brain and spinal marrow, whence the disease is derived, are too remote from the aid of art, more especially if the patient be corpulent; whilst, if the paralysis is not of long standing, and the subjects of it somewhat lean, a complete cure may be obtained.

I have had under my care a great number of

soldiers, who had become hemiplegic from the severe cold which they experienced, during the campaign of Moscow. The Moxa, applied at the sides of the spine, and over the course of the principal nerves of the extremities, produced wonderful effects, in nearly all of them: it is true, however, that the cures took place but slowly.

In my account of the campaign of Egypt, I remarked, that the Moxa restored the action of those muscles which move the upper extremities, and which had been paralyzed by the effect of wounds, although superficial, complicated with injury of the nervous branches of the cervical pairs. I have there also observed, that in relapses of these paralyses, the Moxa should be again applied above the cicatrices, and over the course of the injured nerves: this plan should be persevered in, so long as the chronic state of the disease may require it, whatever may be its character. I shall now relate the case of a young soldier, in whom there was a paralysis of the animal sensibility, only. The circumference of the shoulder—all the exterior surface of the arm, of the fore-arm, and of the right hand, were, in this young man, deprived of feeling: the skin of these parts might be pricked, burnt, or pinched, without his feeling the least pain; whilst the motions of the limb had not been for a moment suspended, but were executed with as much strength and precision, as those of the left. This soldier had received a sabre cut above the clavicle, and in the middle of the triangular space, formed by the junction of the humeral extremity of that bone, with the acromion. The injury was very superficial, and scarcely perceptible:—there was every reason to believe, that the instrument had only touched some ramifications from the cervical branches, destined to form the cutaneous nerves, which are organs of the animal sensibility, whilst those which supply the muscles are deeper seated, and have in truth, another origin, in the spinal marrow.

Some theories, deduced from this anatomical knowledge, are the subject of a memoir, inserted in the collection of the *Bulletins de la Société Medicale d'Emulation*, to which we refer those who are curious to read the account.* Cupping, (*scarifiées*) several times repeated, over the small wound which was healed, and three Moxas applied over the course of the injured nervous branches, were sufficient to restore the sensibility in the whole of the limb, and to put it upon an equality with that of the rest of the

---

* Vide Vol. v. of this Bulletin, 1810. *Author.*

body: in short, this soldier was discharged from the hospital some weeks afterwards, perfectly cured.

Simple and muscular paralysis of the lower extremities, may be the result of concussion of the spinal marrow; or of a certain degree of compression of this medullary production, or of the cauda equina; a compression occasioned by an asthenic turgescence of the spinal membranes, or by the effusion of a serous or sanguineous fluid, into the vertebral canal. In this case, there is no inflammation of the membranes, similar to what we have observed, when the paraplegia is complicated with neuralgia. In the first case, the Moxas alone, are indicated, and even the suppuration should be prevented. The application of this stimulating and revulsive agent, should be made at the sides, and opposite the spinous processes of the vertebræ, descending from the upper extremity of the part in which the disease originates, to the two lateral depressions of the os sacrum. It may also be placed over the course of the sciatic nerves. These paraplegic cases, may be treated with great success, when they are not of very long standing, or complicated with incontinence of urine—a very unpleasant symptom. I am possessed of a great many examples of complete success, obtained by the Moxa in this species of disease; but I shall content myself with relating the following.

Lieutenant General Viscount M****, was struck with a paralysis of the lower extremities, in its second stage, *(porteé au 2de degré)** accompanied with a preternatural jutting out of the last dorsal spinous processes, with deep seated pain in that region, retention of urine, and disposition to *adipous polysarcia*. All the organic and sensitive functions were in such a state of asthenia, that they were very imperfectly performed. Different irritating and rubefacient substances, had been applied, ineffectually to the legs. I was anxious to employ cupping, *(mouchetées)* and afterwards, to have immediate recourse to the Moxa. An elastic gum sound passed into, and left in the bladder, with gentle cathartics, repeated according to the state of the patient, removed the retention of urine, and the obstinate constipation, with which, he had

---

* The author appears to use the word *Degré* somewhat obscurely; as he frequently observes, that a disease had arrived at its first, second, third, and even beyond its third *Degré;* except, however, where he has premised his observations upon any particular affection, by dividing its progress into separate stages: the words first, second, third, and fourth degrees, can only be understood to signify, *figuratively*, its different stages of advancement. *Tr.*

been for a long time, affected. The two first applications of the Moxa caused a sensible improvement, which very much encouraged the General; after the third application, he began to walk with the aid of a stick; after the fifth, without any support; and after the ninth, he found himself perfectly cured—this was in the fourth month of his treatment. This cure is remarkable in several respects.

7.
OF ORGANIC DISEASES OF THE HEAD.

I shall now proceed to enumerate, briefly, the organic diseases, for which, I have also employed the Moxa with great advantage, endeavouring to explain its effects, in each of them. In all chronic affections of the head, I have used this remedy, with the greatest success: thus in idiopathic epilepsy, dropsy of the ventricles of the brain, chronic head ache, &c., the applications should be made all around the basis of the cranium, and especially over the junctures of the squamous sutures of the temporal bone, with the lambdoidal: these junctures in the adult, correspond with the lateral and posterior fontanelles in the fœtus, and very young subjects: it is useless to go higher than the line, which separates the basis of the cranium, from what is called the skull cap *(la calotte)*; and, besides, it may give rise as we have before observed, to unpleasant symptoms; this upper hemisphere being only covered by very thin integuments and aponeuroses, the heat traverses them rapidly, and arrives almost immediately at the membranes of the brain, which it disposes to inflammation, without however, causing any change in the diseased parts of the brain, which are situated so deeply, that the heat cannot reach them. And, in fact, if we consider that the hemispheres of the brain, of a soft, pulpy nature, are five or six inches thick, we may be convinced that the cautery applied upon the top of this mass, can have no effect upon the diseased part, which is commonly situated towards the base of that organ, and, indeed, experience has shewn the truth of this assertion. I shall now cite some rather remarkable examples of cure, obtained by the aid of the Moxa, applied upon the places which have been pointed out.

A young trumpeter, of the chasseurs of the ex-guard, having fallen from his horse, upon his head, was tormented, for about two years, with epileptic fits, so frequent, that he was often attacked twice a day. The cranium was deformed, and it had acquired, in a short time, such a size, that the uniform hat, which he had received on entering the regiment, was too narrow by five or six lines: his eyes were very prominent and almost immovable; the countenance was without color, the pulse slow, and the respiration laborious; the pulsations of the heart were very distant, and scarcely to be felt; and the extremities were almost always cold. Sustentation and progression were performed with difficulty, and all the sensitive functions, especially that of the sight, as well as the mental faculties, were much impaired: in short, every thing announced a compression of the brain, unquestionably concentric, the effects of which were augmented, according to the variations of the atmosphere, or other influencing causes. After a copious bleeding from the jugular,—cupping, upon the nape of the neck, and temples,—the application of ice upon the head,—of mustard baths to the legs,—and the internal use of calomel;—fifteen Moxas were applied round the head, and especially, over the course of the old lateral, and posterior fontanelles. The symptoms were gradually mitigated, so as to render the paroxysms milder, and less frequent; at last, they entirely disappeared, and the patient was perfectly cured before the end of the tenth month of his treatment. All the animal and sensitive functions were pretty quickly re-established; but, what is very remarkable, the arch of the cranium was reduced in its whole circumference; the primitive conformation of these bones being gradually restored: and at the time when the trumpeter was discharged from the hospital, his hat, which was before too narrow, had become five or six lines too large: so that there was a reduction in the whole circumference of the head, of eight or ten lines, which took place under the influence of the Moxa, and which resembled what we observe in the thorax, after the operation for empyema. The effects of this revulsive application round the head, towards the base of the cranium, were powerfully seconded, in my opinion, by the internal use of camphor, in large doses, and of calomel, combined sometimes with the extract of cinchona, with opium, and sometimes with the nitrate of potass and the extract of valerian. The patient, moreover, made use of a decoction of malt, sweetened, and acidulated with muriatic alcohol. This individual was seen, during his treatment, and after his cure, by a considerable number of French as well as foreign physicians, who attended my clinical surgery. Doctor Boisseau, one of the most distinguished of my old pupils, had the particular care of him.

A grenadier in one of the corps of the infantry of the guard, was brought to the military hospital at Gros Caillou, in the first days of the year

1817, having every symptom of a dropsy of the ventricles of the brain; such as evident weakness in the functions of the organs of locomotion, more particularly in the lower extremities; and in all the organs of sense; the sight, especially, was almost extinct, and the voice interrupted and drawling. He had frequent vertigo, and constant dull pains in the head, towards the occiput, with an habitual tendency to sleep, or rather to stupor. The pulse was slow and hard, beating from forty-five to forty-six in a minute; he complained, besides the pains of which we have spoken, of a troublesome weight of the whole head, which he could not bear to bend forwards, or backwards, without being threatened with syncope, which the least neglect, on his part, in not holding it right, brought on immediately. An icy coldness instantly came over all his limbs, and the functions of circulation, and of respiration, appeared suspended together. These phenomena I have frequently had an opportunity of observing in this individual. The mental faculties did not appear to participate at all, in the derangement of the brain; and he could relate with exactness, that his disease arose, in consequence of having plunged, head forwards, into the Seine, from a very high place; and that he had been suffering ever since. After having taken off the fulness of the vessels of the brain, by bloodletting from the jugular vein, and temporal artery, and by cupping *(mouchetées)* on the nape of the neck; ice was applied to the head, and afterwards the Moxas, which were placed upon its posterior and lateral regions: the number was carried to ten, several of which were allowed to suppurate: with these means were joined mercurial frictions to the soles of the feet, every four or five days. After four months of this treatment, the grenadier was discharged from the hospital, in very good health, and returned to his duty; all his functions being restored to their equilibrium. I obtained a like success by the same means, with an Englishwoman, Madame J***, in whom an acute dropsy of the right ventricle, suddenly manifested itself to such an extent, as to strike her with apoplexy, and hemiplegia of the left side, in its second stage. After bloodletting, the application of ice, and blisters to the head, I felt persuaded that the recovery of this lady was ensured; this did not happen, however, until after the fifteenth month, by means of the Moxa, applied towards the basis of the cranium,— between the occipital protuberances,—and upon the sides of the vertebral column. The celebrated JOHN BELL, and Dr. MORGAN, assisted me with their advice, in the treatment of this interesting patient, —the mother of a numerous family.

A child, from seven to eight years of age, son of a retired officer, M. WALTER, and of an

English lady, had every symptom of a chronic dropsy of the ventricles of the brain, with preternatural size of the cranium: he was in danger of dying when I was requested by his father to give him my advice. The first indications being fulfilled, I applied several Moxas upon the nape of the neck, and the sides of the head, which I followed up, some time afterwards, by actual cauteries, placed over the course of the old posterior and lateral fontanelles. The little patient was cured before the end of the ninth month, at which time the cranium, which had been measured before the treatment, was reduced in its whole circumference about six lines. This child at present enjoys perfect health. It is proper to observe, that his sister had recently died of the same disease, as dissection had demonstrated. My brother-in-law, Dr. Coutanceau, attended this little patient for a short time, whilst I was absent.

Since that time another child of the same age, of a scrophulous idiosyncrasy, belonging to M. B***, a merchant at Havre, affected with the same disease, and characterized by the same symptoms—has been also cured by a similar plan: there was in this little subject also, a reduction in the cranium of from three to four lines. Doctors Ribes and Spurzheim were called in, in consultation on this case.

I have also completely cured chronic and rheumatic head-aches, which had resisted a great number of remedies, by the Moxa, applied upon the lateral parts of the head, and the occiput.

This caustic is, in my opinion, contraindicated, in mental diseases attended with exaltation, although it has been extolled in these cases by some authors:—Were I not afraid of wandering from my subject, I should endeavour to explain my reasons for so thinking; for the present, I shall confine myself to observing that it can only be employed in very rare cases.

8.

OF DISEASES OF THE CHEST.

Of ASTHMA.—I have used the Moxa with great success in asthma, when it has not been hereditary, or produced by some malformation in the thorax, and when the subject of it has not been too far advanced in years. I shall suppose also that this affection has for its essential character asthenia of the pulmonary organs, and a spasmodic and convulsive contraction of the pectoral muscles; a consequence of the turgescence or latent inflammation of the vessels of these muscles and the membranes, which are situated on the circumference of the breast; a sort of rheumatic affection, which is commonly occasioned by suppression of the cutaneous perspiration, or other habitual discharges. In accordance with this hypothesis; if the disease has resisted the means ordinarily indicated for restoring the suppressed functions, and putting a stop to the effects of such suppression upon the affected parts; the greatest advantages are to be obtained from the Moxa, the application of which, however, should be preceded by one or more cuppings *(mouchetées)*; the principal effect of this latter means is to take off the fulness of the organic capillary vessels of the skin, and subjacent muscles, and to communicate to the debilitated parts a gentle degree of excitation, which the Moxa gradually increases. The cylinders of the Moxa should be placed in two lines, parallel to the lateral parts of the chest, towards the anterior attachment of the great pectoral muscles, and the costo-scapularis. The number must be relative to the intensity of the disease.

I might relate many cases in confirmation of the success which I have obtained, but I shall content myself with the detail of that of a young Parisian female, who for many years, and after each menstrual discharge, the periods of which, were however, regular, had been afflicted with paroxysms of asthma, accompanied by spasms, convulsive movements, and a sense of suffocation, which were sometimes so violent, that she had been several times in danger of dying.

She was, in the first place, cupped over all the anterior region of the chest; to these local bleedings, which were several times repeated, I added the Moxa, which was placed upon the principal points of the circumference of the thorax. The first applications retarded and diminished the attacks so much, that, considering herself cured, she did not wish to have any thing more done for her; but, suddenly, a fresh and very violent paroxysm came on, which was relieved by the means already mentioned: viz. by cupping, and the Moxa; the application of the latter was particularly insisted upon; and the number of the cotton cylinders, burnt upon both sides of the chest, was carried to twelve. The paroxysms entirely disappeared, and after seven or eight months of treatment, this young lady felt perfectly cured. I had the pleasure of seeing her, some years afterwards, enjoying good health, and without ever having had the least return of her disorder.

Intermittent neuralgic palpitations of the heart, proceeding from debility of that organ, and of the spinal marrow, are successfully combated by the Moxa, which should be applied at the sides of the dorsal column, and round the circle occupied by the heart. I have cured many individuals affected with these neuroses, by the employment of those cauteries.*

9.
OF OLD CATARRHAL AFFECTIONS, AND CHRONIC PHLEGMASIÆ OF THE PLEURA.

The Moxa is equally indicated in old catarrhal affections, and chronic inflammation of the pleura; especially when the disease has been first caused by the repercussion of some gonorrheal or herpetic affection, which is not unusual—or by the presence of a syphilitic virus. According to this supposition, before applying the Moxa, it would be necessary to bring back the repercussed affection, and to remove the virus, by the means which are indicated. I might relate several cases in confirmation of these precepts; but I shall pass on to a much more severe disease, and one which has been a principal object of my researches and meditations.

---

* We ought not to confound these neuroses with the organic diseases of the heart, such as active or passive aneurism of that organ, the curative means being very different.

Author.

10.
OF PHTHISIS PULMONALIS.

Before making a complete memoir upon phthisis pulmonalis, the particular object of which will be, to make known the efficacy of the Moxa, in the cure of this terrible affection, I shall indulge in a short digression upon that disease, which has been considered by almost all authors and practitioners, as incurable and mortal. I might have been convinced, *a priori*, of the efficacy of this application, had I reflected upon the extraordinary success, which I had obtained from its application, in rachialgia, and femoro coxalgia,—which might be more properly termed spinal and articular phthisis, from which phthisis pulmonalis only differs in its seat: in fact, these two affections present the same phenomena, are owing to the same causes, and produce the same effects: besides, it frequently happens that diseased spine accompanies phthisis pulmonalis. In this latter disease, as in rachialgia, the Moxa produces the discussion of the lymphatic congestions, or of the scrofulous tubercles, as well as of those abscesses which are symptomatic, when they are not too far developed. It cleanses the internal ulcers, stops the caries of the bones, and produces the adhesion and healing of the parietes of the abscess, or of the purulent cavities, established in the tissue of the lungs, or in any other part, which may have become the seat of the phthisis. At last, a cure, more or less complete, is obtained, according as the employment of this stimulating and revulsive agent, has been more or less persevered in; an agent, certainly, but little used, but which experience has taught us to be most efficacious in those diseases. The internal remedies, more or less extolled by authors, (even acetate of lead, and, *a fortiori*, the prussic acid) are generally hurtful, or, at least, quite useless: if, however, there should be any particular virus, it would be, first of all, necessary to remove that cause, and, when the phthisis alone remained, to attack it with the Moxa.

Those parts of the chest should be chosen for its application which are most contiguous to the disordered parts of the lungs. The hollow cylindrical tube (the *Pectoriloque*[*] of LAENNEC) will, without doubt, assist us in this research, but the experienced physician has no need of it. Percussion[†], pressure made with care, a little

---

[*] See a *Treatise on the Diseases of the Chest*, translated from the French of R. T. H. LAENNEC, by JOHN FORBES, M. D. &c.   *Tr.*

[†] In almost all cases of thoracic disease, Percussion of the chest, is made use of by the French practitioners; in order to

experience, and the impression of the finger between the ribs, are sufficient to point out, in a manner nearly certain, the seat of the disease.

---

perform this, the fingers of one hand are to be collected into a bundle, so as to have their extremities, upon a level; with these the chest is struck, and the sound produced, carefully attended to by the practitioner. This plan was first recommended by AUENBRUGGER,* a German physician, about the middle of the last century; his work was translated into French in 1770, by ROZIERE DE LA CHASSUGNE,† a physician of the Faculty of Medicine of Montpellier; and by CORVISART, with ample commentaries, in 1808.‡ The principles upon which it has been recommended, are founded upon the difference between the sounds, rendered by Percussion upon the chests of healthy individuals, and of those laboring under disease: for instance, if effusion has taken place into the cavity of the thorax, or any change been produced in the bulk of its contents, the sound is more or less hollow, according to the diminution or increase of the cavity. It will be readily seen, however, that Percussion can only be depended upon, when taken in conjunction with other symptoms; and that its use, under almost every circumstance, cannot assist us much in the diagnosis of any disease: the various conformations of the chest and its contents in different individuals, previous adhesions of the lungs to the pleura costalis, and several other circumstances, may so far modify the sounds occasioned by

* *Inventum novum ex Percussione Thoracis humani ut signo, abstrusos interni pectoris morbos detegendi.* 8vo. Vindobonæ, 1763.

† *De la Percussion de la Poitrine.* Paris, 1770, at the end of the *Manuel des Pulmoniques,* of the same author.

‡ *Nouvelle méthode pour reconnaître les maladies internes de la poitrine par la Percussion de cette cavité. Traduit d'Auenbrugger, avec des commentaires.* Paris, 1808.

In order to put it to the proof, and to leave no doubt respecting the truth of my assertions, I shall relate the history of some cases of phthisis, which I have cured by the Moxa. One of the first persons was a young lady, nineteen years of age, Rosina V****, tall, with hair of a flaxen color, and flat chest: she had an incipient curvature of the spine, with a preternatural jutting out of several of the spinous processes of the dorsal vertebræ—constant pains in that region—frequent cough, with loss of voice—oppression—expectoration yellowish, and purulent—more or less heat in the sternal region, and over the sides of the chest—slow fever, with exacerbations in the evening, followed by night sweats:—all these symptoms announced phthisis, in its second stage, at the least. This lady, reduced to the greatest emaciation, had been affected with the disease for eight or ten months. Many remedies had been tried, but ineffectually.

Thirteen Moxas, applied over the sides of the dorsal apophyses and of the chest, preceded by cupping *(mouchetées)*, repeated at proper

---

Percussion, as to afford no criterion whatever, by which we can be able to judge of the existence or non-existence of organic disease in the thorax.§ *Tr.*

§ Vide Article *Percussion* in the *Dictionnaire des Sciences Medicales*, by MERAT.

intervals, after eight months treatment, completely cured her. This lady has since married, and had two children, which as well as the mother, are enjoying good health.

A second female, of the same age, of small stature, auburn hair, and very much pitted with the small pox, had been put upon several modes of treatment, and had passed many weeks in the Hôpital de la Charité, when I was requested to see her. The left side of her chest was crooked, the scapula jutting out, and the portion of the vertebral column corresponding to it, inclined to the same side, with a continual fixed pain in the part. The cough was almost constant, and frequently accompanied with hemoptysis: she had continued fever, with slight exacerbations in the evening, and night sweats: her emaciation was very great, and the skin without color. The disease had existed for about eighteen months, and the physician who had attended her at the hospital, had considered her as incurable, and that the disease would, in all probability, soon terminate fatally. These symptoms were, notwithstanding, gradually removed, by cupping and the Moxas; the number of which was carried to twenty-one. The incipient gibbosity of the spine, and the deformity of the chest, disappeared also, by little and little, under the influence of this treatment, which was continued, it is true, for nearly two years. The young woman, who had been previously crooked, became straight; her chest was expanded, and she acquired the freshness and *embonpoint*, which we observe in healthy individuals. After having preserved every sign of health, for more than a year, she was suddenly attacked with symptoms of gastro-enteritis, the progress of which was slow and gradual. The parents of the patient, whose means were limited, believing that her disease was of no consequence, contented themselves, without calling in any physician, with the use of some popular remedies, and suffered the disease to proceed. Their daughter was afterwards, however, threatened with such serious consequences, that they decided upon calling in one of my old pupils, Dr. Desrouelles, who very zealously made use of those means which were indicated; but, notwithstanding the most rational and attentive treatment, she died of marasmus, a few weeks after the invasion of this latter disorder.

On dissection, we found the left lung, in which the phthisis had been situated, in a healthy state, and that it had contracted a great many adhesions, by membranous expansions, with the pleura costalis: we observed, also, in many parts of its parenchyma, contractions, or species of deep cicatrices, where, without doubt, during the disease, so many purulent cavities had been situated. The whole mass of the viscus was reduced by one third of its natural size. The cavity which contained it, was sensibly narrower than the other, and its parietes were very much sunk in. This work of reduction was the effect of the cure. We observed in the right lung, a single tubercle, excavated by a vomica *(un foyer purulent)*, of some lines in diameter. The peritoneum and intestines were in a state of suppuration, as well as the mucous membranes of these viscera.

A third person, also of the same age and sex, H. B. upon whom nature had lavished all her favors, was threatened with imminent danger, from a very advanced phthisis. It had even been declared, at the last consultation held upon her case, that nothing more could be done for her, in consequence of the advanced state of the disease, and her extreme weakness. Being anxiously solicited by her parents to take her under my care, I yielded, with some difficulty, to their reiterated entreaties, and undertook the treatment of her, in September, 1817.

I shall dispense with relating the symptoms of the disease, and shall merely observe, that the young patient was in a state of slow continued fever, with exacerbations in the evening—flushings of the cheeks—painful and frequent cough—

expectoration of yellow grayish and viscous matter, and of a purulent appearance—she had oppression—extreme debility—slight aphonia—pain between the shoulders, and in the sides—the tongue, the roof of the mouth, and the inside of the throat, were covered with aphthæ, or excoriations, which appeared to extend into the air passages—and the nails of the fingers were crooked. Twenty Moxas, preceded by a few cuppings, *(mouchetées)* and a seton, placed in the left side, had removed the symptoms, and conducted the patient by degrees to an unexpected cure. The treatment had continued eighteen months, and she enjoyed perfect health. But since the time when I wrote out this case, and after a whole year passed in this satisfactory condition, she was attacked, from several fresh causes, with an inflammation of the bowels, of which she died, notwithstanding all the means we could make use of, and the most assiduous and attentive treatment: she did not, however, exhibit a single symptom of her former disorder.

The subject of the fourth case was a Belgian, named P****, thirty-four or thirty-five years old, of a brown complexion, and very irritable habit, who was certainly laboring under a confirmed phthisis pulmonalis, which had existed about two years.

The principal symptoms of this disease, were a frequent and painful cough, with an hemoptöe which came on daily, and sometimes so copiously, that it constituted a true hemorrhage *(une veritable hémorrhagie)*: it was preceded by a febrile attack, by heat in the chest, redness of the tip of the tongue, and of the cheeks, and was followed by an icy coldness of the extremities, by syncope, and an almost total loss of pulse, so that he was several times in the greatest danger; to the foregoing symptoms, were joined a total loss of voice, with deep aphthæ over all the mucous membranes of the mouth, of the nasal fossæ, and probably also, of the larynx and pharynx: no particular virus existed in this case.

Notwithstanding the almost desperate condition of the patient, and the unfavorable prognostic, which several physicians who had been called in, in consultation, had given; I ventured to undertake the following treatment, the basis of which, was the successive and repeated use of cupping *(mouchetées* and *scarifiées)* upon the back and chest, and of fifteen Moxas, which were left to suppurate slightly.

After the application of the thirteenth Moxa, the hemoptysis was arrested, and never afterwards returned. All the other symptoms gradually disappeared, and the patient set out for his usual residence, having been under treatment between seven and eight months. His health was pretty quickly re-established, and his *embonpoint* reproduced in the same proportion. His voice alone remained feeble. One of the physicians consulted, M. LAENNEC, who, from the beginning, had pronounced the existence of extensive ulceration in both lungs, having explored the whole circumference of the chest, a second time, and with the same instrument, made himself satisfied of the cicatrization of the ulcerated parts, and confirmed the cure of the patient.

The subject of the fifth case was a young female, twenty-seven years of age, a milliner, who was affected with advanced phthisis pulmonalis. She was in a confirmed state of marasmus, with continued fever, nocturnal fœtid sweats, and constant expectoration of purulent matter: the catamenia had been suppressed for a very long time, and the uterine passage was almost totally obliterated; it would scarcely admit the introduction of a very small elastic-gum sound: besides the chief symptoms of phthisis, there was, between the posterior edge of the right scapula and the dorsal spines, a round tumor, formed by the preternatural curvature of the posterior extremities of the third and fourth ribs, between which, a deep and obscure fluctuation might be felt. The most gentle pressure upon this part caused the most acute pain, extending to the under part of the clavicle of the same side. This pressure excited violent cough, accompanied with a copious expectoration. The motion from coughing communicated an impulse to this part, which could be easily distinguished under the finger; and without having recourse to the cylinder of LAENNEC, we could easily discover that the lung of this side was deeply and extensively excavated.

It was not until after the repeated entreaties of the parents, that I determined upon taking this patient under my care: and I was anxious to know if, in this very advanced disease of the lung, the Moxa would have effects similar to those which I had obtained from its use in diseased spine, when almost in its last stage. Before employing the Moxa, I was nevertheless anxious to have my diagnosis confirmed by my colleague, Dr. LAENNEC, who as well as myself, with the assistance of his *Pectoriloque*, detected the cavity of which I have spoken. Notes were taken of this consultation, at which Doctors RIBES and DESROUELLES formed part. In short, the Moxa was immediately applied, beginning at the tumor, round which, six were successively placed; thence I passed to the other regions of the chest, which I considered to be most in relation with the internal ulcerations. To my great surprise, the two first relieved the pains and the spasm, and produced sleep, which she had not been able to taste for more than six months. This sensible amelioration encouraged me, and I continued its application under suitable modifications, until the fifteenth. The projecture in the dorsal region formed by the ribs, gradually disappeared—the cough became easier—the expectoration diminished, and became of a better appearance—the appetite was restored—in short, the patient went on improving, until she was able to leave her bed and walk about her chamber; and soon afterwards, to walk out for hours together. She had been under this treatment for about fifteen months, when I engaged M. LAENNEC to see her again; he satisfied himself, as in the case of M. P. that the deep cavities which I had mentioned as existing in the whole of the superior and posterior lobes of the right lung, were obliterated and cicatrized. In consequence of feeling so very well, she was desirous of going into the country; to this I consented the more willingly, as her residence at Paris was unhealthy, and very inconvenient for her *promenades*. During the first days she felt pretty well, she had gained some flesh, and had but little cough; but having been exposed, during a stormy night, to the external air, which shifted suddenly to the north-east, she was struck with very violent gastro-enteritis, which obliged her to return to Paris, and notwithstanding the employment of local bloodletting, and all the usual antiphlogistic means, this young lady died about the fifteenth or seventeenth day from the invasion of this disorder, and in the ninth month of the treatment for the phthisis.

On opening the body, we found the right cavity of the thorax considerably narrowed; the upper half of the lung shrivelled, firm in some parts, and traversed by membranous adhesions; the lower portion was sound, but numerous membranous adhesions had taken place, between it and the pleura-costalis. The bronchiæ of the left lung were filled with a mucous purulent matter, and we found some small vomicæ, in the substance of the lung. The mucous membranes of the stomach, and intestines, were inflamed, and covered with gangrenous spots.

This dissection confirms the correct prognosis of LAENNEC, and exhibits the advantageous effects of the Moxa, in every stage of phthisis pulmonalis—as, in this case, it had deterged the ulcerated cavities, and produced cicatrization.

The subject of the following case was more fortunate, and although his disease was equally far advanced, he obtained a complete cure. He was one of the vergers of the King's Chapel, at Versailles. This man, who was of a phlegmatic habit, and about twenty-seven or twenty-eight years of age, was in the second stage of tubercular phthisis, when he requested my advice, at the beginning of the year 1818. All the glandular system of the neck was swollen, and the face without color; he felt great oppression, and was tormented with a troublesome and almost constant cough, followed by an expectoration of a greyish fœtid matter; the mucous membranes of the throat, and of the entrance of the pharynx, were covered with aphthæ; deepseated pains were felt in the back, and in the sides of the chest; and there was a disposition to continued fever, with evening exacerbations, followed by abundant sweats—in short, he was in a state of marasmus.

The cause—at least the predisponent cause of this disease, appearing to me to be owing to the presence of a particular virus, I administered the means which were required for the removal of this morbid cause, at the same time that I applied the Moxas. These derivative applications were placed, by two at a time, at relative intervals, and at fit opportunities, upon both sides of the dorsal spine, and upon the lateral parts of the chest:—the number was carried to thirty-six. This treatment was continued about fifteen months, when it was followed by a complete and unexpected success. All the functions, in this patient, were gradually re-established: he recovered his *embonpoint*, and, at this time, enjoys perfect health.

A young English lady, Mary J***, possessing the most agreeable *Physique*, along with every mental accomplishment, and the sweetest disposition—has been also so fortunate, as to be cured of a like disease, in its first stage: only half-a-dozen Moxas were here required for the cure. I have since received several letters, from this young person, which shew that she still continues well.

I shall confine myself to the detail of those facts, which appear to me to be sufficient for drawing the attention of practitioners, to the efficacy of this cautery, in the case of phthisis pulmonalis.*

---

* I should also have spoken of the advantages which may be derived from this application in dropsy of the pericardium, and in hydrothorax, if I had not already mentioned the circumstance in different memoirs, inserted in my *Campagnes*, and to which I refer my readers: I should observe, however, that this remedy can only produce a cure, when the diseases are in an incipient state; an observation, the truth of which, I have had different opportunities of proving. *Author*.

11.

OF CHRONIC & ORGANIC DISEASES OF THE ABDOMINAL VISCERA.

1st. Of the STOMACH.—Congestions in the coats of this viscus, and scirrhus which is commonly a consequence of them, constitute a severe disease, which has almost always a fatal termination; and experience has taught me, that every internal medicine is completely useless or hurtful: this circumstance has caused these disorders to be considered incurable, especially if the swelling at the pyloric orifice has arrived at such a degree, that the food passes with difficulty, or is rejected by vomiting. I can affirm, however, that even in this condition, the disease has yielded, in many cases, to the repeated application of the Moxa upon the epigastrium, the combustion of which should be carried on by means of the blow-pipe, as in phthisis, so that the heat may penetrate more deeply. In order that the value of this stimulating and revulsive application may be better appreciated, I shall proceed to relate some cases, the subjects of which had been laboring under chronic turgescence, already far advanced, of the pyloric orifice of the stomach; at least, I had every reason to believe so, from the nature of the symptoms.

One of the first patients, affected to the degree which I have just mentioned, was the valet-de-chambre of General RUTTY. He felt a dull, constant pain in the region of the stomach, with eructations of an acid nature, and of a disagreeable smell. He had frequent nausea, and a few moments after having taken his food, vomiting supervened, and continued for a longer or shorter time. The alvine evacuations were few, scanty, and of a hard matter, unless, when from the effects of some cathartics, of which he made frequent use, by the direction of physicians, a flux supervened, to a greater or less extent, which was sometimes followed by diarrhœa. He was in a state of slow continued fever, and in the greatest degree of emaciation; when he lay down upon his back, an oval tumor of the size of a hen's egg, situated transversely, and in the region of the pylorus, could be felt through the abdominal parietes, which were very much extenuated; pressure upon this part, gave considerable pain. The liver also appeared to project beneath the edge of the false ribs, and I considered, that the spleen and mesenteric glands, were likewise in a certain degree of obstruction. The abdomen was covered with large varicose veins, and the skin of the whole body was of a dingy color, and dry and scaly.

This valet, aged forty, had been in the last

campaigns in Spain, Russia, and Saxony, during which, he was exposed to the intemperateness of the seasons, and to different climates; to these circumstances we may refer the exciting causes of this disease, being in all probability predisposed to it by some particular morbid principle. After having been cupped, *(mouchetées)* several times on the hypochondria, back, and epigastrium, I began the application of the Moxa upon this last region, and persevered in its use, until the twenty-second time, with the proper modifications which I have mentioned in other circumstances. This treatment continued fifteen or sixteen months, at the expiration of which time, he felt perfectly cured; all his functions were gradually restored to their former state; his *embonpoint* soon re-appeared, and he enjoys at present (two years after his cure), good health.

I might also relate the cases of several other subjects, who were afflicted with similar diseases in different degrees, and who have, in like manner, been restored to health by the same means.

2dly. Obstructions of the liver, spleen, and every other abdominal viscus, may be treated with equal success by the Moxa, more especially when the disease has not arrived at its greatest degree of developement.

I shall relate a single example of chronic hepatitis, accompanied with abscess, which was brought to a favorable termination, by the application of the Moxa.

The subject of this case, was a *Conducteur* of one of the *diligences* from Paris to Rennes, named FERLURA. This man, who was about forty-five years old, had complained for seven or eight months, of dull pains in the right side of the chest, which was much more prominent than the left; he was in a state of obstinate constipation; a dense and slightly painful tumor, was readily perceptible, below the ribs of the same side, in the bottom of which, the patient experienced slight shooting pains. A physician was called in, who applied a hemlock plaster over the tumor, and prescribed gentle cathartics; but the disorder making progress, I was called in, in consultation. The disease was then at its highest pitch, the whole of the hypochondrium was very prominent, and there was beneath the margin of the false ribs, an oval tumor, of about the size of a fist; it was hard round its edges, and a deep-seated fluctuation could be distinctly felt, towards the centre. Mercurial frictions had been made use of to the tumor, and the physician had recommended that a trocar should be plunged into its centre, in order to give issue to the purulent matter that (there was every reason to suppose) existed in the tumor, which certainly presented every indication of an hepatic abscess. Before opening it, however, it was agreed that the Moxa should be applied around it, and that no other topical means should be made use of.

After the second application of the Moxa, the tumor had evidently diminished in size externally, but the deepseated and lancinating pains which he experienced, had augmented, and he had also considerable repugnance to the application of any more Moxas; I, however, removed his objection, and three more cylinders were used, at an interval of two or three days. After the fifth, the patient experienced a violent attack of cholic, which was followed by repeated alvine evacuations, at first, of a bilious matter mixed with pus, but afterwards, entirely purulent, the quantity of which might be estimated at about a pound; these evacuations were succeeded by a total disappearance of the tumor in the hypochondrium, and of the internal lancinating pains, which he had incessantly experienced until this time.

It is very evident here, that the Moxa had caused the developement of the adhesive inflammation, which had unquestionably begun between the inferior paries of the abscess, and the corresponding part of the transverse colon, the coats of which had ulcerated, and the pus been immediately discharged into that intestine. I have reason to conclude, that the Moxa is an excellent remedy for promoting the resolution of congestions in the liver, and even for favoring the exit of the pus from hepatic abscesses, into some passage which may conduct it to the exterior.

I saw in Egypt an hepatic abscess, which burst spontaneously into the transverse colon, and was evacuated by the bowels. *

A third individual, affected with an hepatic abscess, was treated in our hospital by the same means: in this person, the evacuation of the pus was likewise made by the bowels. The case was collected by one of my pupils.

3rdly. A salutary revulsion may be also produced in chronic congestions of the uterus, which are almost always followed by cancerous ulcerations, from the application of the Moxa upon the lumbar regions, preceded by cupping *(mouchetées)* upon the same parts, and by a depurative treatment. By these means, I have

---

* See vol. i. of my *Campagnes.*

baffled this disease, and, in several cases, prevented its invasion, when there were strong threatenings of it.

I shall now proceed to treat of the phthisis of the bones, or of that asthenic, rheumatic or scrofulous affection, which commonly attacks young people, in the fibro-cartilaginous and osseous parts; such as the spine, the junctions of the bones of the pelvis, and the articulations of the limbs.

12.

OF RACHITIS.

The principal effects of rachitis, are a softening of the bones, and a bending or deviation from the right line of the vertebral column, along with a greater or less gibbosity. The Moxa is, without contradiction, the remedy *par excellence*, for this disease. Ancient and modern authors, and especially POUTEAU, have passed the highest eulogiums upon it; and the illustrious DESAULT taught us to observe, that the success of this remedy is more certain, when, contrary to the opinion of the celebrated surgeon of Lyons, the wounds or burns, left by the Moxa, for the reasons which I have already given, are not suffered to suppurate.

With this latter intention, ammonia must be applied immediately after the Moxas have been consumed. The application of this cautery must be repeated, as often as the state of the disease may require it.

The Moxa may be employed in every period of the disease; it is better, however, to make use of it in the first stages, and before the deformity has reached a very high degree. We should avoid applying it over the spinous processes of the vertebræ, for fear of causing a denudation and caries of these bony points; the application should be made, as much as possible, over the course of the posterior branches of the vertebral nerves, between the transverse processes, so as to allow a communication at the same time, with the spinal marrow.

Corsets, or other mechanical means, unless they are employed as retentives, or as simple supports, are in this case, more pernicious than useful; the curvature or jutting out of the bones, may, it is true, be repressed to a certain extent, but if the morbid process continues, the disease shews itself, towards those parts which are diametrically opposite, and affects the intregrity of the functions of the internal organs.

We ought then to proscribe the use of these

machines, and to confine ourselves to that of Moxa, and of those internal remedies, which are considered to assist its effects. The intervals of its application, should be proportioned to the age and strength of the patient; it is better that the treatment should be protracted, than that the individuals should be exposed to inflammatory symptoms, or to the effects of a symptomatic fever, produced by a great number of Moxas, the applications of which, have been too frequent. I could relate a great number of examples of success in these cases, from the application of this cautery.

13.

OF RACHIALGIA.

The Moxa is, above all, imperiously indicated in tabes dorsalis. I shall permit myself to make a slight digression upon this most severe disease, the effects of which have been considered fatal, by almost all physicians. It has been designated under the names of Vertebral Disease—Curvature of the Spine—or Disease of POTT: (see vol. iii. of that author's works.) Notwithstanding the remarks and interesting cases which that surgeon has given, respecting this disease, we are not commonly aware of its existence, until it has arrived at its second or third stage; a time at which the assistance of art is less successful, than when employed at the invasion of the first symptoms.

Until the time of POTT, we had only vague and uncertain notions respecting diseased spine: the effect was often confounded with the cause: and, even at the present day, authors and celebrated practitioners, consider the symptomatic abscesses, which are certainly the result of caries of the vertebræ, as a disease isolated, and independent of that of the spine.*

The researches which I have made, during thirty years passed in camps, and in military hospitals, have enabled me to confirm the principles of that celebrated English surgeon, and to minutely analyze the phenomena which this disease presents in its different stages. My numerous trials have likewise made known to me a sovereign remedy against it, in the reiterated application of the Moxa. This is the principal subject of what I am about to relate. I have considered it right, in the first place, to reform the improper phraseology, under which the disease of which we are treating has been designated, until the present time; and to substitute for it, a name which may make known its true

---

* See BOYER's *Pathologie*.

character;—as it consists in an inflammatory condition of the vessels of the fibro-cartilaginous and osseous substance of the vertebral column, or of the bony substance of other parts of the trunk, I shall name it according to its seat: viz. Rachialgia, when it attacks the spine—Sacro-coxalgia, when it is situated in the sacro-iliac symphyses—Sternalgia, when in the sternum—Costalgia, when upon the ribs or their cartilages—Scapulalgia, when in the scapula—and Femoro-coxalgia, when it is seated in the coxo-femoral articulation.*

I designate under the name of rachialgia, that rheumatic or scrofulous affection, seated in some part of the vertebral column, the principal effect of which is, to produce a latent or chronic inflammation, in the fibro-cartilaginous and

---

* It will be readily seen, that the different names which Baron LARREY has given to this affection, according to its seat, are perfectly insufficient for the conveyance of any knowledge, respecting its " true character;" the words—Rachialgia, Sacro-coxalgia, Sternalgia, &c. according to their derivation, merely signifying pain in the spine, sacro-iliac symphysis, and sternum, without conveying any idea respecting its nature. As, a minor, but not unimportant circumstance also, this nomenclature is liable to objection, in consequence of its inelegance, in a classical point of view; one part of the word, in many of the instances, being derived from the Latin, whilst the other has its origin from the Greek. *Tr.*

osseous tissues of the vertebræ: this is a true phthisis. This inflammation, far from augmenting, by turgescence, the volume of the parts, weakens their tissue, and appears to accelerate the work of absorption and of decomposition; so that the bodies of the vertebræ, where the disease first fixes itself, becoming softened, sink down by degrees; the spinous processes tend to separate more from each other, and make a projecture behind, or are depressed forward, or deviate to the right or the left, which circumstances characterize gibbosity in its different senses; the intervertebral cartilages, are the first to be decomposed or dissolved; and to this loss of parts from absorption, erosion, or caries in the corresponding parts of the osseous substance, soon succeeds, where it developes itself with more or less rapidity, according to the intensity of the causes, or to the age and idiosyncrasy of the patient;—the caries seldom attacks the spinous or transverse processes.

From the first moment of the erosion, there is an emission of a serous purulent fluid, from all the injured vessels, which accumulates, at first, under the membranes, or the surrounding ligamentous fasciculi *(trousseaux)*; afterwards infiltrates or diffuses itself, in the cellular membrane, towards the depending parts, or towards those where it meets with the least resistance, and accumulates in points more or less distant, where it produces what we designate under the name of symptomatic abscesses, or abscesses *par congestion*. These abscesses, as the English author has judiciously observed, are constantly the result of the caries, or one of its principal effects. The progress of these abscesses varies *ad infinitum*: most commonly they are situated in the dorsal or scapular regions: the matter spreads through the interstices of the muscles, at the insertion of the tendons, and at the transverse processes—accumulates in sacs, formed by the aponeuroses, or the large muscles of the back— sometimes passes under the pillars of the diaphragm—follows the direction of the psoas muscles, and collects in the fold of the groin, or passes through the pelvis, and gains the nates; in other cases, it follows the direction of the ribs, and proceeds to form collections in the anterior part of the chest: in short, nothing is more extraordinary than the progress of these *fusées*, and the developement of the abscesses which are occasioned by them: this circumstance should render the practitioner very circumspect in his prognosis, as well as in the employment of the means which he adopts.

The first symptoms of this disease are deep-seated local pains, at first, somewhat obscure; these, afterwards, increase, and extend into the course of the spinal marrow, and of the nerves which emanate from it, especially into those which go to the members nearest the seat of disease; the muscles of these parts are struck with stupor, without being paralysed; the limbs experience painful cramps, and a sort of stiffness or accidental retraction, with a sensation of coldness, independent of the temperature of the air; to these symptoms are joined lassitude, oppression, loss of appetite, emaciation, slow fever, with intermissions, more or less irregular, followed by a colliquative flux, and marasmus.

I shall enter into a more detailed account of the progress of this disease, in speaking of the femoro-coxalgia—an affection of a similar nature, which attacks the coxo-femoral articulation; and shall only remark here, that the caustics made use of by Pott, against rachialgia, have not the advantages which I derive from the Moxa.

The abundant suppuration which these first caustics furnish, without producing the revulsion which we desire, weakens the patient considerably, especially if symptomatic abscesses exist. If these same abscesses are opened early, (whatever may have been the method adopted) before employing the means which are effective against the caries, the patient quickly dies.

Now, in the administration of those means, we must direct our attention to the prevention of any foci of suppuration, from being established; it is sufficient to produce an excitation upon the affected parts, in order to divert the morbific principle, and to alter the vital properties of the inflamed parts.

The Moxa, preceded by cupping *(scarifiées)*, if necessary, perfectly fulfils this double indication. I shall now content myself with pointing out the causes of the disease of POTT, and to make known my mode of treating the abscesses, *par congestion*, which are its principal effect.

The causes of rachialgia, are a rheumatic or scrofulous *vice*, and, in general, every thing which can contribute to annihilate the vital powers of the vertebral structure. This affection developes itself and proceeds slowly, but it is seldom that it stops in its course, and gets well spontaneously. It is one of these diseases, of which nature cannot rid herself, without the assistance of art, and the consequences of which are commonly fatal. We should therefore hasten to employ those means which are the most proper for combating the morbific cause; and experience has taught me that the most powerful and efficacious remedy is the **Moxa**.

A great many subjects, who had been considered in a desperate state, have owed their safety to the employment of this *heroic* remedy. I shall, in the first place, relate the history of several cases, which prove the truth of this assertion, and shall afterwards have occasion to revert to the theory of the disease.

CASE 1.

General L ****, much reduced from several debilitating causes, was attacked with a tabes dorsalis, with slow fever, notable asthenia of the genital organs, curvature of the spine, stiffness and numbness of the lower extremities—marasmus in its first stage. This affection had withstood a great many means. It was decided in consultation, that a series of Moxas should be applied upon the vertebral column, and the region of the sacrum, without discontinuing the use of cinchona and chalybeates, which had been administered until that time. A favorable change occured, after the three first applications; the strength was re-established in proportion as the applications were repeated: at the seventh M. L. could walk alone, and at the thirteenth, he was able to go to the mineral waters, for the purpose of completing a cure, which was already in a very advanced state: —he has made several campaigns since.

CASE 2.

Mademoiselle D***, about twenty-five years of age, was in the first stage of marasmus, with well marked symptoms of phthisis pulmonalis: the dorsal vertebræ were already curved backwards, and to the right: the scapula of the same side was detached from the trunk about three centimetres (In. 1.181) by a soft tumor, or incipient *Dépôt par congestion:* this symptom indicated the first stage of a vertebral caries: in short, the young patient was proceeding with rapid strides towards the termination of her career, when I was called in, in order to give her my advice.

The debilitating regimen, upon which she had been kept for many months, was replaced by one that was tonic and nourishing. Cinchona, combined with opium, and balsamic and gummy substances, were prescribed. Twenty Moxas were applied successively, at intervals of three or four days, at the sides of the spinous processes of the dorsal vertebræ, opposite the spaces which separate the transverse processes. The first favorable change was the almost sudden cessation of the symptoms of the phthisis pulmonalis, and soon afterwards the reduction of the projecture of the dorsal vertebræ, and the diminution and resolution of the subscapulary tumor, as well as the subsidence of the scapula: the general strength was gradually re-established, and the internal organs resumed the play of their functions:—in short, the young lady is at present enjoying good health.

I shall now give an account of a disease nearly similar to the preceding—it is the history of the case of one of the patients at the Military Hospital at Gros Caillou.

CASE 3.

JOSEPH RICHAULET, aged twenty-three years, one of the foot artillery of the Guard, in February, 1816, had a tumor of the size of two fists, and of an oval form, situated behind the spinal edge of the right scapula: it extended from the base of the spine of that bone to beneath its inferior angle: there was a fluctuation in its whole extent, and it was without pain, or change of colour in the skin: he continually held himself crooked: the spinous processes of the dorsal vertebræ were jutting out, and separated from each other; and this portion of the spine deviated a little to the left (the side opposite the tumor): when the region corresponding to these vertebræ was slightly pressed upon, a sharp pain was felt, accompanied with a sensation of sinking, which amounted almost to syncope, when the pressure was prolonged. This tumor, and the other symptoms which accompanied it, made me easily recognize the Disease of POTT, in an advanced stage: it was the sequel of a rheumatic affection, which he had contracted in the frozen and wet bivouacs of the campaign of France in 1814. The condition of the patient was so desperate, that I did not expect any success from the employment of the Moxas: I nevertheless tried them: at the third application, which I made at about two or three days distance, upon the course of the dorsal vertebræ which appeared the most affected, he found himself relieved, and the tumor had slightly diminished. At this time I had a sketch taken of him.* I prescribed antiscorbutics, and the Moxa was continued until the twenty-fourth: the last were applied upon the external paries of a purulent sac, which prevented the union of the parietes of the tumor. The cure of this soldier was completed on the 23rd of July last.† During the course of his disease, he experienced a shortening of about two centimetres (In. .787) in his stature.

---

* See the plate in vol. iv. of my *Campagnes*.

† See the same Work.

This patient was presented before the society of the Faculty of Medicine, before and after his cure.*

In Vol. ii. page 396 and seq. of the history of my *Campagnes*, several other cases may be found, which prove the successful employment of the Moxa, in rachialgia, or tabes dorsalis, accompanied with caries and abscesses *par congestion*, produced by it.

After having made use of the Moxa until the progress of the disease was arrested, I have opened the abscesses in some cases, after the manner mentioned in the work before cited, which consists in making an oblique opening, by means of a narrow knife, heated to whiteness; and then, immediately evacuating all the purulent matter accumulated in the abscess, by means

---

* Lady MORGAN, in her work upon France, testifies her astonishment at the remarkable cures obtained in cases of this kind by the assistance of the Moxa: a remedy at this time never used in England. (Vol. ii. appendix 3rd.) *Author.*

It may seem astonishing, that the author should quote the testimony of Lady MORGAN to the cures obtained by the Moxa: that astonishment will, however, cease, when it is recollected that her husband, Sir CHARLES, is a physician, and that the appendix to her work relating to the state of medicine in France, was written by him. *Tr.*

of dry cupping, and a lightly compressive bandage.

The following case, and those which are related in my other work, as they shew this mode of proceeding more in detail, will, without doubt, justify the precepts which have been laid down.

CASE 4.

PIERRE MOUSOT, aged twenty-four years, of a bilious phlegmatic constitution, fusileer in the sixth regiment of the Royal Guard, contracted, in the cold and wet bivouacs of the campaign of Saxony, towards the end of the year 1813, a rheumatic affection, which fixed itself in the back. After having been assuaged by rest and a better regimen, none of the symptoms remained, to which this affection had given rise, with the exception of some periodical pains, which had settled about the same part; when, during the winter of 1815, they recurred with greater force, and in May, 1816, he was removed from the fever wards, where he had been undergoing an anti-rheumatic treatment, into mine. There was at that time, a considerable tumor between the spine and the posterior edge of the scapula. I discovered, at the first inspection, the disease of POTT in its third stage, characterized by gibbosity, by deviation of the spine towards the left side, and by paralysis of the body of the bladder, and of the inferior limbs.

The dorsal tumor* was of an oval form; it was about twelve centimetres (In. 4.724) in its greatest diameter, and projected to nearly the same extent; the fluctuation was uniform over the whole surface, and the skin presented no change of color.

I began the treatment by the application of cupping, both dry and *scarifiées*, over all the course of the vertebral column, which I followed up by the Moxas and the usual medicines.

A favorable change was the effect of the first applications, which continued to make progress. The tumor however, the volume of which had undergone a very marked diminution after the fourth application, but less sensibly from that to the twenty-first, remained stationary until the 25th of July, when a little phlyctena suddenly appeared in its centre, which gave us reason to expect that the abscess would soon break spontaneously: under this conviction, I hastened to plunge into it a knife with a narrow

---

* See the Work above cited.

blade, heated to whiteness, so as to make an incision of about a centimetre and a half (In. .594) in length, beginning at the phlyctena, and directing it towards the lowest part of the tumor; a vessel of about the capacity of a litre (Pints 2. 1133) was soon filled with a serous and inodorous matter, of a greyish white color and mixed with albuminous flakes; a cupping glass applied over the opening, completed the removal of the little fluid which remained at the bottom of the cavity; in the remnant of the fluid, we found some friable osseous grains, which I believed to be the *detritus* of the carious portion of the body of one of the vertebræ.

This operation threw the patient for four days into a state of extreme weakness, which I treated by an antiseptic potion and a strengthening regimen; a febrile attack shewed itself afterwards, by repeated shiverings, followed by intense heat; it was accompanied with a feeling of painful constriction in the hypochondriac regions, with dyspnœa, slight colic, diarrhœa and tenesmus; the tongue was furred, and of a reddish purple color; and the urine scanty, and of a reddish brown.

There was reason to believe that from the aberration or metastasis to all the mucous membranes, of the very acrid principle of the suppuration, furnished by the caries of the bodies of the vertebræ, a chronic inflammation had established itself in all these membranes, which gave rise to the symptoms, of which I have just spoken.

The use of cupping *(mouchetées)*, of large blisters upon the thorax and abdomen, and the administration of mucilaginous anodynes, removed the imminent danger, and replaced him in a favorable state. Finally, in order to favor the adhesion between the parietes of the purulent sac, I again applied the Moxa.

On the 25th November, 1816, he might be considered as nearly cured: he walked with tolerable freedom, but was deprived of the power of bending his trunk forwards, or sideways, in consequence of an union between the bones primitively affected by the caries: his stature was diminished about four centimetres (In. 1.574). It is evident, in this patient, who was perfectly cured after two years treatment, that the caries of the cartilages, and of the bodies of the vertebræ must have been very extensive, as there was so great a loss of substance.

Another mode of procedure would have been still more advantageous, if the fluid contained in the abscess had spread into a portion of the cellular membrane, which communicated deeply with the purulent cavity;—this would have consisted in passing a seton through the cellular membrane; the fluid would immediately pass out through the wounds of the seton, and continue to drain out gradually, until it was entirely evacuated. If the caries of the bone which had furnished this fluid, was then arrested, as we have supposed in this case, the complete cure of the patient would have been the more certain, from the matter of the abscess having been gradually evacuated, and without any communication having taken place, between the external air and the purulent cavity. Two cases, the details of which will be given hereafter, have been advantageously treated after this method.

CASE 5.

THOMAS, fusileer in the fifth regiment of the Guard, aged twenty-two years, after repeated bivouacs, and frequent attacks of rheumatism, had several times experienced acute pains, which in the summer of 1816 again occurred, principally in the upper part of the back. There appeared, at the same time, between the left scapula and the superior dorsal vertebræ, a tumor, the progress of which was rapid and remarkable; as, fifteen days after its appearance, it had acquired considerable size,* and presented a manifest fluctuation on every part of its surface: the superior portion of the dorsal spine projected considerably forwards, so as to form a concavity behind. This condition, which is very uncommon, was, doubtless, owing to the diseased state of the posterior part of the bodies of the vertebræ; so that the spinous processes approached each other, whilst the anterior part of the body of each vertebra, tended to remove itself from the corresponding part of the bone, above and below it. The superior extremities were in an almost complete state of paralysis.

Twenty cupping glasses and thirteen Moxas were successively applied round the tumor, in the space of two months. In proportion as these applications were multiplied, their efficacy was the more evident—by the diminution of pain, and reduction in the bulk of the tumor, as well as by the return of motion in the thoracic members. On the 20th of November, the tumor was reduced to one quarter of its former size, and the patient was in a way to convalescence. This soldier, having been discharged, returned home, where the cure will, without doubt, have been completed.

---

* See the Work already quoted.

CASE 6.

DULARD, cuirassier of the Guard, after having been exposed to the pernicious influence of the frozen bivouacs in Russia, was attacked with a fixed pain in the lumbar region, along with remarkable numbness, and very marked debility in the lower limbs, which were subsequently affected with almost complete paralysis.

The physicians of Bourbonne-les-Bains, to which place he had been sent, did not perceive the nature of the case, and only treated him for the paralytic affection—but to no purpose.

When he was brought to our hospital, I discovered, from the symptoms which have been already several times mentioned, a well marked rachialgia. The three first lumbar vertebræ formed a gibbosity of about three centimetres (In. 1.1811): the slightest pressure upon this part caused acute pain, as well as slight convulsive movements in the lower extremities. At the first application of the cupping glasses, which was repeated in five or six days, over the whole spine, the hypochondria, the flanks, the buttocks, and the thighs, the relief was so evident, that he allowed me to begin the employment of the

Moxa, and to substitute, for the refrigerants which he had been taking until that time, tonics, administered under modifications suitable to the indications.

Fourteen Moxas, applied successively upon the sides of the gibbosity, and towards the dorsal and sacral regions, conjoined with cupping *(scarifiées)* caused it totally to disappear: they re-established the contractile action in the extensor muscles of the lower limbs, which were more especially affected with paralysis, and facilitated progression, as well as the play of all the functions, to such a degree, that on the 20th of November he was in a way of cure, and went out of the hospital a few weeks afterwards.

CASE 7.

LABAUDRE (BLAISE) aged twenty-eight years, soldier in the first regiment of the infantry of the Royal Guard, after having given way to incontinence, began to feel, about six years ago, pains in the back and pelvis.

When he was transferred, on the 7th of September, 1817, from the Military Hospital of Val de Grace, where he had remained about six months, to that of Gros Caillou, he presented in the left inguinal region, an abscess *par congestion*, of an oval form, of the size of two fists, with an evident fluctuation in its whole extent, and without any change in the colour of the skin: already one of the most prominent points of the abscess was about to open; and it was accompanied with pains in the haunch and thigh of the same side, as well as in the dorsal region.

A manifest gibbosity, of about two centimetres (In. .7874), formed by the separation of the spinous processes of the last dorsal vertebræ, proved that at the Hospital of Val de Grace, they had mistaken the primitive disease, of which the abscess was only symptomatic; as this tumor had arisen in a carious part, established in the bodies of some of the dorsal or lumbar vertebræ. Cupping, both dry and *mouchetées*, applied upon the whole extent of the dorsal region, and especially upon the sides of the gibbosity, combatted the chronic inflammation, and relieved the patient.

After the application of nineteen Moxas, the tumor, which had at first diminished a little in size, remaining stationary, and the point, of which I have spoken, appearing again about to open, I passed a seton through the integuments and cellular membrane of the groin of the same side; taking care to comprehend in the perforation, the deep cells of this region, with which the purulent matter, shut up in the sacs, appeared to me to communicate. In causing the matter to be evacuated gradually, and in an indirect manner, I was desirous of shunning a direct opening of the tumor, on account of the softness and trifling thickness of its parietes, as well as from its vicinity to the abdominal viscera. Notwithstanding, however, the very marked reduction of this abscess, its parietes were so extenuated, as to make me afraid of its spontaneous opening—this circumstance made me determine to plunge a red hot knife into it, after the manner which I have described above.

During the three first months which followed the operation, the patient was as well as could be expected: the suppuration, although abundant, was of a good quality—the symptoms of fever from absorption were dissipated—all the functions were well performed—and LABAUDRE began to walk about the ward: but this unfortunate person, being accustomed to spirituous liquors, abandoned himself to them without moderation, so soon as he found himself out of danger, and in a way of cure; in consequence of which, he was attacked, a few days afterwards, with violent colics, ardor urinæ, and, subsequently, with a comatose affection. The suppuration from the wound, which had remained fistulous, was suppressed, and a *metastatic* absorption, towards the lungs and the brain, shewed itself almost immediately; the functions of these organs became disturbed and gradually weakened: in short, after a month of anguish, he died from marasmus and exhaustion.

Twenty-four hours after death, we proceeded to open the body, the color of which had already become livid:—the limbs were flexible, and the viscera of the thorax and abdomen presented nothing remarkable: the cranium was not opened, but we had reason to suspect a purulent taint of the brain, from the paralytic state of all the muscles of the extremities before death, from the symptoms of cephalalgia and of mental aberration which also manifested themselves before the total extinction of life. After having removed the viscera of the abdomen, we discovered, as I had affirmed at the time when the patient entered the hospital, a purulent cavity which extended from the fistulous wound in the left iliac region, along the psoas muscle and behind the peritoneum, to the bodies of the second and third lumbar vertebræ, in which a loss of substance of four centimetres (In. 1.574) in thickness was observable; this was formed at the expence of these two vertebræ, the two remaining portions of which had approached nearer each other, and entered into a mutual adhesion. The cavity which resulted from the loss of substance, was re-covered by the ligamentous *surtout:* ossific vessels, sent off from each of the two portions, had formed two little bridges upon the sides, whilst the central parts tended to approach, in order to form a similar union. The sketch of this pathological specimen may be seen in the fourth volume of the work already cited: it proves in an incontestible manner, that caries of the vertebræ, however extensive it may be, can be arrested, and that the parts decayed by this ulceration may cicatrize, as happens in venereal caries of the cranium, when treated methodically.*

* I have had under my care three soldiers, who, in consequence of constitutional syphilis, had a caries in several points of the cranium, which destroyed, in one, the whole thickness of the external table, and of the diploë of the frontal bone: in the other, it had extended its ravages even into the sinus of that bone, causing a great loss of substance: the third, in short, had the frontal and the occipital bones in a state of caries:—at present, all three are enjoying perfect health. The loss of substance, or the cavities occasioned by these caries, are perceptible to the eye and touch, under the integuments which have contracted an adhesion at all points. The Moxa is not indicated in this kind of caries; it accelerates its progress, unless the cause of it be destroyed, or combatted at the same time by specific means.

I shall not terminate this note, without speaking of the treatment which I have adopted in syphilis, and which is employed with the greatest success, in the hospital, the surgical

It is evident that the caries in LABAUDRE had been arrested: that the bony portions

---

direction of which, has been confided to me for nearly twenty years. This treatment, which I distinguish into internal and external, consists in the administration, internally, of a compound of oxymuriate of mercury, muriate of ammonia, and extract of gum opium, in equal parts: six, eight, or ten grains of this compound, dissolved in a proper quantity of Hoffman's anodyne liquor, is sufficient for a litre (Pints 2 .1133) of sudorific syrup, or of distilled water. The syrup may be given in the dose of from half an ounce to two ounces. The second preparation* is administered in doses of from two drachms to an ounce, in some proper mucilaginous liquid, such as milk; mercurial frictions of from one to three drachms made constantly on the soles of the feet, at three or four days interval, which we follow up by soap washes and exercise, constitute the external treatment. *Author.*

* By the *second preparation*, the author most probably alludes to the solution of the oxymuriate in distilled water, instead of in the sudorific syrup; and yet this seems to be unintelligible, as each solution contains the same proportion of active ingredients. The sudorific syrup used by the author, was, in all probability, formed from the sarsaparilla; or, according to the formula for the *Syrupus Depurativus*, or *Sirop de Cuisinier*, which is used as the vehicle for the administration of the oxymuriate of mercury, by a great majority of the French practitioners: (See *Nouveaux Elémens de Thérapeutique, &c.* par J. L. ALIBERT, Tome ii. p. 275:)—This syrup is made in the following manner—

℞
    Sarsaparillæ, ℔ii.
    Florum Boraginis, ⎫
    ———— Rosarum, ⎬ ana ℨii.
    Sennæ, ⎭
    Anisi,
    Sacchari, ⎱ ana ℔ii.
    Mellis, ⎰

Fiat secundùm artis regulas syrupus, cujus singulæ libræ addi potest murlatis

destroyed by the affection had been cicatrized and re-united with each other, and, as occurred in the subjects of the preceding cases, that there wanted nothing more to form a complete cure than the detersion of the purulent cavity, which had disorganized the cellular tissue of the psoas muscle, and of the iliac region where the abscess appeared.* This fact proves, in short, that these diseases are curable, when we have courage to persevere in the employment of the Moxa, and when we are careful, in the opening of the

---

hyperoxidati mercurii granum unum. Dosis communis, uncia una vel altera, (See ALIBERT, *Ibid*, p. 651).

It appears also more than probable, that the Author alludes to some syrup similar to the form which has been just given, as CADET DE GASSICOURT in his *Formulaire Magistral*, amongst his Formulæ, gives the Sirop Dépuratif du Dr. LARREY, which is made as follows:—

"Take of
Syrup of Sarsaparilla,
—— de Cuisinier, } of each one Litre (Pints 2.1133.)
Corrosive Muriate of Mercury,
Muriate of Ammonia, } of each gr. 20.
Extract of Gum opium,
Hoffman's mineral liquor, ʒii.

This syrup is given, in the dose of an ounce, in the morning, fasting, in a cupful of decoction of sarsaparilla, (See *Formulaire Magistral* par C. L. CADET DE GASSICOURT, 2de Edition, 1814, Paris, p. 265.)—The whole of the note, however, is very unsatisfactory, as the author has neglected to inform us of the extent to which he carried his treatment. *Tr.*

* A soldier of the second Swiss regiment of the Royal Guard, is now under treatment by the same means, at the hospital of Gros Caillou, for an affection which presented the same symptoms; he is in a way of cure. *Author.*

abscesses, which are the result of the caries, to empty at once all the matter contained in the sac, unless we make use of the seton. I shall terminate this paragraph by the detail of two cases, which are extremely curious.

CASE 8.

BULLIARD (JEAN-JOSEPH) aged about twenty-one years, of high stature, fair complexion, and lymphatic constitution, soldier in one of the Swiss regiments of the Royal Guard, was received into the military hospital of Gros Caillou, December 6th, 1818, for the purpose of being treated for abscesses *par congestion*, which had shewn themselves for some months: the most considerable was situated in the dorsal region, and the second upon the highest portion of the sternum: the left knee of this patient was swollen, and the motions of this articulation were very contracted: the ninth, tenth, and eleventh dorsal vertebræ jutted out somewhat considerably; and the least pressure made upon the spines of these vertebræ, caused the most violent pain: he was emaciated, pale, and there was a febrile disposition, accompanied with slight remissions, &c.

From all these symptoms I acquired a conviction, that this young Swiss was affected with a phthisis of the bone, with abscesses *par conges-tion*, seated in the bodies of the last dorsal vertebræ, in the sternum, and at the femoro-tibial articulation. This disease, already arrived at its second degree, was doubtless caused, by the scrofulous idiosyncrasy of the patient, and by onanism, to which he had given way without reserve.

After some days observation, I prepared him for the Moxa, the application of which appeared cruel to him at first; but he became gradually accustomed to it, and at last suffered all the necessary applications to be made, with the greatest courage, and with perfect immobility. I occupied myself, at first, with a treatment proper for the sternal tumor, round which I caused twenty Chinese Moxas to be applied: I afterwards opened the symptomatic abscess, which was of the size of a large hen's egg, by means of the caustic potass.

The purulent matter being evacuated, the cavity became cleansed, and on the sternum a carious spot was observed, which had given rise to the abscess. This decayed part became deterged; small particles of the compact laminæ of the bone exfoliated, cicatrization took place, and the ulcer of the soft parts, which remained for a long time fistulous, also healed subsequently, like the carious portion of the bone, under the salutary influence of fresh Chinese Moxas, placed all around.

The dorsal tumor had acquired, during this time, such a considerable bulk, that it equalled the size and form of a child's head. I placed upon the sides of the vertebral column, beginning at the superior part of, and around, the tumor, thirty cotton Moxas, which were consumed by the aid of the blow pipe: the first having relieved him much, he was encouraged to suffer its application to be continued. Pills of extract of hyoscyamus, of nitrate of potass, and camphor, and some particular precautions, caused the pernicious habit which he had contracted to disappear; and I was enabled to continue the treatment with security, and with all the success which could be expected from it.

The abscess in the back appearing stationary, and the most prominent part threatening to break; when he had arrived at the thirtieth Moxa, and after four months treatment, I decided upon operating according to my own method, viz. with the hot knife: I chose one of the days for my clinical attendance to perform this operation, which was followed by the evacuation of about three pints of liquid, similar to that, which the opening of the abscess of LABAUDRE had furnished us. The dressing being finished, I took every necessary precaution to prevent or dissipate the consecutive accidents; a treatment, analogous to that of the preceding patient, after some trouble, conducted the disease to the end which I was desirous of attaining: he went on improving, and, after a year's treatment, found himself, with respect to the rachialgia, in a way of cure.

But the tumor of the knee had augmented in like proportion, notwithstanding the use of all the means indicated. I did not wish, however, to remove the focus of this morbid process, before the rachialgia had been entirely cured, as I had done with regard to this latter, which I did not attend to until the sternalgia was removed; I then continued to give my care and attention to the dorsal disease until the time of its cure, which was very far advanced at the end of the spring of the year, 1820. The disease of the knee having made very great progress, and feeling convinced that the caries had attacked deeply, all the articular parts, I then decided upon amputating the thigh, which the unfortunate individual had himself requested for some time. This operation, although performed with precision and method, was followed by a frightfully conic stump. Many surgeons who attended my lectures on clinical surgery, felt persuaded that I should be obliged to have recourse to resection —but I removed their fears. Experience had taught me that this projecture, being the effect of local irritation, and of the wasting away of the cellular tissue, would cease, when the exfoliation of the osseous *virole* which occurs at the end of the divided bone, to a greater or less extent, should take place, and that there then would be no more cause of irritation; because the motive fibre being re-swollen, and separated by the unctuous fluid which again fills the cellular tissue, nature gently draws back the soft parts towards the end of the stump, and restores them, and the divided part of the femur, to a perfect level: so that resection, so much praised by some authors, and by many practitioners, is not only useless, but may be dangerous; it is useless—because it is difficult, not to say impossible, for the saw to fall precisely above the points of the sequestrum, which the necrosis produces in the cylinder of the femur, at distances more or less removed from its end: and if ever so little of this sequestrum, or dead osseous matter were to escape, nature and art would have as much trouble in producing its separation, as that of the whole sequestrum. As for the danger from resection, it will be proportionate to the hemorrhage or inflammation of the fibrous membranes which may accompany it. All these considerations will be developed in a particular memoir upon this accident. This phenomenon occurred, in a very evident manner, in BULLIARD and one of his comrades, whose thigh I had likewise amputated, for a like disease, and in whom the portion of the bone affected with necrosis, having once exfoliated, the soft parts of the stump put themselves upon a level with the sound part of the bones, and the cicatrix was accomplished: at last, this person went out of the hospital perfectly cured, in the first days of the month of August, 1820. He has lost about three centimetres (In. 1.1811), in height; his *embonpoint* has returned, and there is every reason to suppose that this soldier, who has now returned to his country, with the subject of the following case, is enjoying good health. This case is remarkable in several respects.

CASE 9.

The success, which I have obtained in the subject of the following case, is not less astonishing, although the disease has no affinity with that of the preceding: I shall proceed to give its history, because the Moxa has moreover, contributed much to the safety of this soldier.

STOBLER (LOUIS) aged twenty-one years, one

of the soldiers of the first Swiss regiment of the Royal Guard, in a paroxysm of nostalgia, threw himself from the third story of his barracks, with the intention of breaking his limb, in order that he might be disbanded and sent home: the result of such a fall, the principal effect of which was concentrated in his right leg and loins, may be imagined beforehand; this limb was shattered in its lower third; and the first lumbar vertebra was luxated forward, upon the last vertebra of the back.

The deep depression which was perceptible behind, upon this part—the preternatural projecture, which occurred immediately, above the spinous process of this last vertebra—the sudden and complete paralysis of the lower limbs, of the intestines, and the bladder—the great pain, and icy coldness of death—left no doubt respecting this luxation; and although I had founded no hope of preserving this young soldier—after having brought him to, by the proper means, I endeavoured, as much as possible, to fulfil the indications which presented themselves.

I directed, first of all, several series of cupping glasses *(mouchetées)*, to be applied upon the lumbar regions, and upon the whole of the surface of the lower belly: I afterwards enveloped him in the still smoking skin, of a sheep recently killed. This application I followed up by embrocations of very hot camphorated oil of camomile. Every attempt at reduction would have been useless and hurtful. Two bleedings in the arm, and a third in the jugular, in order to dissipate the effects of the concussion, which had been violent, were successively practised, and he was put upon the use of refreshing and antispasmodic drinks.

Although the comminuted fracture of the leg indicated the amputation of this member, I deferred it from the little hope that existed of his recovery; and I contented myself with the application of the dressing, of which I make use in cases of this nature. Having, however, recovered the use of his senses, and passed the first five or six days without any increase of the severe symptoms which I have just mentioned, I conceived some gleams of hope of saving him, by a continuation of the treatment, and by assiduous attention. The paralysis of the limbs and of the abdominal viscera, was carried to so great a degree, that he experienced no painful sensation in his limbs, notwithstanding the fracture and the slight burns which were made, in order to prove his insensibility. The retention of urine had already been remedied, by means of an elastic gum sound, which was suffered to remain in the bladder. But none of the purgative clysters administered, had been able to remove the obstinate constipation, which this poor young man had experienced, from the time of his fall. It was necessary not only to clear out the intestinum rectum, of the hardened matters which filled it, by means of a scoop made on purpose, but I was also then obliged to reach, with the scoop, the sigmoid flexure of the colon, which was equally filled, at the point where it makes its angle in the left iliac region, across the parietes of the abdomen. After twenty days of this treatment, along with tonic frictions or embrocations, made over all the surface of the body, there was a sensible amelioration, and the excretions began to be restored: there still, however, remained great weakness in the lower extremities, and fixed pains in the region of the luxated vertebra. I then began the use of the Moxa, which I applied by two at a time at the sides of the last dorsal and first lumbar vertebra. The number was carried to eight: the sensibility and the muscular motions of the lower limbs, were pretty quickly re-established under its influence; so that after eighteen months treatment, the patient would have been able to walk, had it not been for the state of deformity, and contraction of the fractured foot and limb. He then solicited the amputation of the limb, which I had already judged indispensable. I performed this operation in the thickness of the condyles of the tibia, as the disease extended very high; nothing interfered with the healing of the wound of the stump, the cicatrix of which was linear.

The motion and the animal sensibility of the parts, which had remained a long time paralyzed, were progressively restored, and the patient, after having walked with some difficulty with the assistance of crutches, perfectly fulfilled this function with his wooden leg. In short, at the end of two years and a half, he obtained a perfect cure. He was about four centimetres (In. 1.574) shorter, than when he entered his regiment. The false ribs are only a finger's breadth from the crest of the ilium, and a deep depression still exists beneath the spinous process of the last dorsal vertebra, which is itself very prominent. This is the third example which I have seen, of a luxation, which I believed complete, of one of the last dorsal or lumbar vertebræ, produced suddenly by mechanical causes. The two first are inserted in my *Campagnes*, the subjects of which ought to be at the Hôtel Royal des Invalides. The curious phenomena which the last cure presented to me, will form the subject of a memoir, which I purpose to make upon these luxations, at a future opportunity.

14.
OF SACRO-COXALGIA.

Rheumatism may attack the sacro-iliac symphysis, so as to produce, in young persons more especially, a gradual disunion of the two bones, and consequently, a sort of spontaneous luxation; it is, indeed, the only one of the articulations of the bony system, where such a species of spontaneous dislocation can occur; it is true, however, that it is generally produced by a mechanical cause, such as falls, or strong compressions exercised in a direction, contrary to the line of union between the two bones. This luxation may also occur in very young women, who have been recently delivered of children of a disproportionate size: of this I have seen examples; I have even been obliged to cause a young lady, seventeen years old, to wear a retentive and compressive bandage, in whom, after a laborious accouchement, a separation of the ossa ilii from the sacrum had taken place, similar to what occurs in the females of the *Cobayæ* during parturition. The symphyses were nevertheless gradually reunited, and this lady has since gone on well.

The case, communicated to the Academy of Surgery, towards the end of the eighteenth century, by M. LHERITIER, professor of the practical school, is a striking example of this affection. The subject of it was a young husbandman, who, after having suffered a long time from a rheumatic pain in the right sacro-iliac region, experienced, in consequence of a fall, such a separation of the two bones which form this symphysis, that the ilium moved upwards and downwards, alternately and reciprocally, with the greatest facility. M. LHERITIER, after having made use of the actual cautery, ingeniously thought of fixing the two portions in apposition, by means of an elastic bandage, the form and composition of which may be seen in the sketch which has been made of it, and which should be in the archives of the Faculty of Medicine in Paris. I have since seen, in young soldiers, this mode of dislocation occur suddenly, from the oblique action of spent balls, upon the hip bone, from above downwards. I might here relate, *en detail*, the case of a patient, laboring under a similar infirmity, which I had under my own eyes, a short time ago, at the Hospital of Gros Caillou.

In this affection, the corresponding abdominal limb experiences a preternatural elongation, proportionate to the abasement of the hip bone, if the dislocation of this bone takes place from above downwards; in the contrary case, the limb presents a shortening, equally preternatural, and proportionate to the elevation of the hip bone. It is difficult to establish the diagnosis of this particular derangement; the local pains, however, being augmented by immediate pressure, and the manifest tumefaction in the sacroiliac region, are sufficient to satisfy us of its existence.

It often happens that this disease produces, in the symphysis which unites the ilium to the sacrum, a carious process, similar to that which affects the vertebræ, as I have mentioned in treating of rachialgia, and towards the coxo-femoral articulation, in the femoro-coxalgia, of which I shall soon speak.

If the disease be recent, we may remedy it by the means adopted by Professor LHERITIER, to which may be advantageously added, the reiterated application of the Moxa. If the disease be of long standing, and especially if improper union of the bones have occurred, the disease is incurable.

The means indicated in rachialgia ought to be employed in this affection, which is of the same nature; but I cannot too strongly recommend, that the application of the Moxa should be avoided, upon those portions of skin which immediately cover the bones: the space, therefore, must be chosen, which corresponds to the diseased symphysis, as is pointed out in plates No. 3 and 4, of the fourth volume of my *Campagnes*.

The same kind of affection, sometimes also attacks the sternum, the ribs, or the scapulæ, as I have seen it:—the result of this disease, when established in the substance of one or in many of these bones, is precisely the same as in the preceding cases. It may be equally affirmed, that the abscesses, which shew themselves at points more or less in proximity with the focus of the disease, are constantly produced by the caries of one of these bones. Nor do these abscesses differ as to their nature and developement, from those which accompany rachialgia, properly so called. We might give to these affections the names of Sternalgia, Costalgia, and Scapulalgia.

In these disorders, as in rachialgia, I have remarked, in every case, that where the opening of the abscess, when it occurs spontaneously, takes place, before the caries of the bone, which produces it, is stopped by the means which I have made known, it is constantly mortal; whilst if we make early use of the Moxa, so as to arrest the progress of the caries, the operation, pointed out for these abscesses, is attended with fortunate results; of which I have seen a great number of examples.

15.

OF FEMORO-COXALGIA.

I call by this name, the latent or chronic inflammation, which establishes itself in the fibro-cartilaginous and osseous structure of the coxo-femoral articulation, similar to that of which I have just made mention, and which attacks the vertebral structure and the sacro-iliac symphysis. It is commonly the effect of a rheumatic affection, or exhaustion of the prolific powers of the individual.

This disease may be hereditary, acquired, or scrofulous—rarely syphilitic. It is necessarily hereditary, when it is the result of a scrofulous *vice:* it is this species which we see in children. With this supposition, the means which I shall proceed to point out, for combatting the rheumatic femoro-coxalgia, a disease which is always accidental, are generally indicated with few modifications, for the same disease, when of a scrofulous nature. The symptoms, moreover, which accompany this affection in infants, are the same as those produced by the rheumatic femoro-coxalgia in adults, who have been exposed to causes which produce and cause the developement of the rheumatic affection. I shall confine myself, then, to the description of this latter affection, reserving some reflections upon the effects of the scrofulous femoro-coxalgia, until the end of this article.

Rheumatic femoro-coxalgia rarely attacks the extreme ages: it manifests itself commonly from the first epoch of puberty to the commencement of manhood; that is to say, at that period of life when the work of ossification is nearly terminating. The developement of this disease is made with the more facility and promptitude, according as the subjects are exposed to an *ensemble* of vicissitudes, the effects of which bear upon the fibrous and ligamentous systems. Young soldiers, subjected to the laborious marches of armies—destined to long campaigns, and to peragrate cold climates, are the most liable to it: I observed this particularly at the termination of the long and distressing campaign of Russia.

In the major part of these young soldiers, the disease being very far advanced, and having been at first mistaken, terminated fatally: I have had the happiness, however, of treating several of them, with an unlooked for success.

Before relating the cases of these individuals, I shall succinctly describe the symptoms of femoro-coxalgia.

It declares itself by pains more or less deep in the articular region of the femur; they are soon propagated along this bone to the articulation of the knee; where they concentrate in such a manner as to turn the attention of the patient, and of the physician, from those which are felt towards the ilio-femoral articulation: this circumstance has occasioned many errors.

The individual generally carries his thigh and leg half bent: the motions are executed with difficulty, especially those of flexion and complete extension of the limb; and its nutriture quickly becomes impaired.

In the first period, the extremity lengthens by degrees, and passes the level of the other. This preternatural elongation is owing to a state of relaxation and paralysis, into which the muscles, surrounding the joint, fall, and to turgescence and inflammation of the synovial membrane; it may be also attributed to a similar state of the ligaments, and especially of that which fixes the head of the femur into the bottom of the cotyloid cavity, upon the point of insertion and substance of which, more particularly, the rheumatic *vice* carries its first effects, as well as upon the synovial apparatus, which fills the sigmoid fossa of the articular cavity. During this first period of the morbid process, the pains are deep-seated: the patient experiences general uneasiness, and the functions of internal life are more or less disturbed, according to the irritability of the individual: a febrile attack establishes itself, with intermissions, more or less perfect, according to the duration of the attacks: these *epiphenomena* might be explained by the stagnation of the fluids which lubricate the articulations, and by the latent inflammatory state of the capsular ligaments, of the synovial membrane, and of the bony parts of the joint. The cartilages, by their swelling, do not thrust out the head of the femur, as several authors have written, (see vol. xv. page 33, of the *Dictionnaire des Sciences Médicales*) for I have constantly found them, on dissection, rather lessened and dissolved, than tumefied; their organization not admitting of tumefaction.

By this state of general disorder of the articular parts, the head of the femur becomes removed by degrees from the bottom of the cotyloid cavity, and an elongation of the limb is produced, the more sensible, from the articular ligament having lost all its elasticity, or being detached from its point of insertion, either at the bottom of the cotyloid cavity, or at the head of the femur, which happens very early. In fact, when this ligament is separated from one of its points of attachment, the femur, by reason of its curvature and gravity, tending to resume a right line, necessarily produces in the whole of the limb, an elongation, so much the greater, from the powers which concur to fix it in its relation with the hip, having lost their spring.

But—Is the head of the femur entirely displaced, as the same authors have advanced; or, if it is not, what does happen to it?

Before it has arrived at the edge of the cotyloid cavity, erosion of the inter-articular ligament, and of the diarthrodial cartilages takes place; and unless from a fall, or forced movement of the thigh, capable of displacing the articular extremity of the femur, then deprived of its ligament of insertion, and, consequently, readily admitting of luxation, it does not occur spontaneously: and if, on dissection, we find the head of this bone displaced, to the outside of its cavity, we should ascribe the essential cause to a fall, or to a violent percussion, the effects of which have borne upon the extremity of the bone, in such a manner as to produce a primitive or consecutive luxation. The femoro-coxalgia may have preceded or followed this luxation:

and this must have been the case, in my opinion, with those patients who were the subjects of the cases of SABATIER, my distinguished master, (See *Les Mémoires de l'Académie Royale de Chirurgie.*)

When luxation exists conjointly with the disease of which I am speaking, it is attended, along with the symptoms proper to femoro-coxalgia, by those which characterise luxation; an occurrence which I have never met with, in the great number of patients whom I have had under my care. But the process of internal erosion is accompanied by a serous, lymphatic effusion, which fills, first of all, the cotyloid cavity, and, doubtless, concurs to the removal of the head of the femur, the dimensions of which are reduced by the caries which attacks its surface. It invades, at the same time, the whole extent of the articular cavity, perforates even, sometimes, the thinnest parts; extends, by degrees, into the os ilium; penetrates into the pelvis, where the fluid, which at first accumulated in the articulation, proceeds suddenly to form purulent *fusées*; whilst, at other times, it separates the fibres of the capsular ligament, filters into the interstices of the neighbouring muscles, and forms one or more abscesses, in points more or less distant from its source. From this time, the symptoms become more intense; the limb may even undergo a momentaneous shortening, owing to the wearing away, from the caries, of the head of the femur, or to the sudden passage, from the articular cavity, of the fluid contained therein: this characterizes the second period. This phenomenon, when it has taken place, has given rise to the belief of a spontaneous luxation; but in examining attentively, the rectitude and conformation of the member, we do not find any signs, which unequivocally characterize this luxation: and I repeat, that, unless from a concomitant mechanical cause, the head of the femur, already moreover reduced by the caries, does not luxate. I have never seen a single example of it, although I have had occasion to open the bodies of a great number of persons, who have died from the effects of femoro-coxalgia.

The third period is characterized by the progress of the caries, the developement of the abscess externally, in points more or less distant from the seat of the disease, as well as by a febrile and cachectic state of the system. These abscesses are nearly circumscribed, and present an uniform fluctuation in every part of their surface, without local pain, or change of color in the skin; they increase slowly and insensibly, and when they have arrived at their last stage, the parietes become thin, and at last open spontaneously. From this time, he falls into a state of slow and colliquative fever; a gangrenous affection strikes the ulcerated parts, and the patient dies. On dissection, purulent foci are found around the articulation, and the bony parts are destroyed by the caries.

Such is the progress of this disease, which I have attended to, in a great number of individuals. When it has not passed the first or second period, it is capable of cure; especially if the patient be removed from the action of the causes which have produced it. I have seen many cases of it, and several are related in my *Memoires et Campagnes*. I shall make known others, in the course of this article, not less interesting. But if the disease has arrived at the third period, it is much more difficult to arrest its progress, and to obtain a cure: nevertheless, we may and should try the use of indicated remedies;—I shall now proceed to make known these remedies, and their mode of application. In the first period, we should divert the inflammation from the articular parts, by local derivative bleedings, such as cupping *(scarifiées)*, around the articulation, which may be repeated several times. By this operation, performed *à propos*, we disgorge, successively, the vessels of the articular ligaments; the pain diminishes, and the patient experiences manifest relief. If the inflammatory symptoms continue, or if they recur, during the progress of the disease, which has happened to some of my patients, a seton should be passed, in the fold of the thigh *(dans le pli de la cuisse)*, through the integuments and cellular membrane, without either touching the muscles, or any of the crural vessels and nerves. I have employed this plan, with advantage, in one of the subjects of the cases which follow this article—The Moxa produces, afterwards, the most advantageous effects.

" Quibus a diuturno coxendicis dolore femoris " caput suo loco excidit, iis crus tabescit et " claudicant, nisi urantur." HIPP. Aph. 60. Sect. 6, Edit. Bosquillon.

Dr. CORREF, one of the learned Professors of Berlin, had the goodness to inform me, at the time of his journey to Paris, in the beginning of 1816, that Professor RUST, of Vienna, now Professor in the university of Berlin, used the red hot iron with great advantage, and without any preparatives, which he applied over the articulation, and in three oblique lines uniting at the great trochanter. M. RUST has caused a cautery to be constructed, for this purpose, the form and thickness of which are such, that it preserves, during the whole application, the quantity of caloric, necessary for producing, with a single stroke, the desired cauterization, without being obliged to replunge it in the fire: he has observed, that immediately after this cauterization, the limb suddenly returns to its natural length, and puts itself on a level with that of the opposite side: I have had occasion to verify this remarkable phenomenon in several cases, (the histories of which will be related hereafter) and in which it was reproduced, as the German professor has described. This phenomenon may be explained, I think, in the following manner—by attributing, in the first place, as I have observed, the elongation of the limb to the rupture of the inter-articular ligament, at one of its points of insertion, as well as to the state of paralysis of the surrounding muscles: the application of the actual cautery upon the articular region, must needs produce, immediately, a simultaneous and almost tetanic contraction of these muscles, and recal, in the weakened ligaments, the elasticity and spring necessary for fixing the head of the femur temporarily in the cotyloid cavity, whither it is suddenly drawn back by this artificial contraction. What confirms still farther the assertion advanced, respecting the rupture of the inter-articular ligament, is, that if the patient, believing himself cured, because his limbs have recovered their level, should make use of any exertion, which may be sufficient to bring back the rheumatic affection into the muscles, and by consequence the species of paralysis which is the result of it, the limb lengthens again almost immediately, and preserves this new elongation for a greater or less time, if by fresh excitants the action of the muscles, and the elasticity of the ligaments, be not re-established. These principles will be confirmed by one of the cases which are at the end of this article. The sudden contraction by the application of the cautery, proves incontestibly that there is no luxation. But I have also observed, that when we confine ourselves to the employment of the metallic cautery, the limb again becomes gradually elongated, and the symptoms of the disease, which had for the moment disappeared, soon return; this recurrence may, however, be prevented by the reiterated application of the Moxa; and by persevering in its use, we succeed in curing the disease.

Now ought it to be said, that the application of the actual metallic cautery is needful, or useless. Without presuming to pronounce upon this question, which experience alone should definitively resolve, and although the remedy is terrific, I think that it may powerfully assist the success of the Moxa, which, from not acting with the same energy, does not arrest, so promptly, the progress of the disease.

The Moxas should be applied round the articulation, by one, or, if the strength and courage of the patient will permit it, by two at a time. An interval, of one or more days, should be left, between the applications, according to the effects obtained, or to the state of the atmosphere: foggy, or wet and cold weather, does not answer so well as dry and serene.

FIRST STAGE.

In the first stage of the disease, it is easy to conceive in what manner the means which I have just pointed out, may arrest its progress, and restore the vital properties in the parts affected. Cupping, by taking off the fulness of the engorged vessels, of the fibrous and bony structure of the joint, favors the circulation of the fluids in these vessels, and re-establishes the suspended functions of the lymphatics: the effects of the irritation and inflammation, then gradually abate.

HIPPOCRATES knew very well the good effects of the employment of cupping, in what he called hip disease, as the following passage from his book *de Locis in homine*, proves:—" Quum " Coxendicum Morbus à fluxione fiat, cucurbitam " medicam affigere oportet, &c." The advantages of cupping, shall be shewn at another time, more in detail, in a particular article, appropriated to that curative means.

The combustion of the Moxa, carried on by the blow-pipe, should be preferred to that which is performed spontaneously, without the aid of the breath; because, in the first case, the column of air, which is made to pass with force through the capillary tube of the blow-pipe, conducts, or transmits to certain depths, along with a great quantity of oxygen, the matter of the caloric, which the combustion disengages; and it is to the excitation which this double igniferous principle produces, deeply, in the affected parts, that the efficacy of the remedy is owing. Moreover, at each application the Moxas divert the internal irritation, and the mass of caloric, which they communicate to the most profound parts, augments their spring, and restores them to their primitive state.

SECOND STAGE.

If caries has begun, and there is a purulent collection, these means have a less prompt and efficacious action: they frequently, however, succeed, as I have had opportunities of observing; which should encourage practitioners, to make use of them, and to persevere in their employment.

This second stage of the disease, is characterized, as I have observed, by great elongation of the limb; difficulty in moving it, or even total immobility; by extreme emaciation of the patient, and by slow fever. Sometimes the causes, mentioned above, may produce in the limb, a shortening more or less sensible; the circumference of the articulation is painful to the touch, and tumefied towards the depending parts, where sometimes a fluctuation, and incipient *depôts*, near to, or distant from the articulation, may be distinguished. In these cases, cupping is less indicated; we should hasten to apply the Moxa. The actual cautery should not be employed, except with the greatest precautions; in order that the parietes of the abscess may not be divided, if it is pretty near the articulation, because their opening would establish a communication between the external air and the purulent cavity; from which unpleasant symptoms might arise; especially if the carious process were not arrested, as I have already observed. The violent but gradual excitation, which the Moxas communicate to the diseased parts, arrests the morbid process, and appears to augment the action of the absorbents, so that the fluids, already accumulated in the abscesses around the articulation, or in those which are more or less distant from it, (provided they are not too much distended) are taken up, and transmitted into the circulating mass. I am ignorant of the channels by which the absorption of this matter is accomplished; but I think that it is by the cellular tissue, and the venous system: in all cases it is marked by a diminution of the tumor, by a pustular eruption,* which shews itself over the whole body, as well as by an earthy and purulent sediment in the urine, which is constantly precipitated, on standing, to the bottom of the vessel.†

Caries, or ulceration of the bones, may cicatrize, and really does cicatrize, leaving, like ulceration of the soft parts, a depression proportionate to the loss of substance, and an expansion or developement of the vessels of the bone, which pass from the edges of the caries towards its centre, in order to produce its cicatrization. If the caries had attacked the bony parts which are in con-

---

* We know that a cutaneous eruption, similar to flea-bites, frequently marks the termination of rheumatism. *Author.*

† We read in the *Mémoires de l'Académie Royale des Sciences*, the case of a young person, who was completely cured of a gibbosity, after a fever of ten days, and several purulent dejections. *Author.*

tact in the articulation, the limb would have remained shorter than the other, with deformity and lameness.

Whatever may be the effects of femoro-coxalgia, it is very rare that nature unites the osseous articular pieces together: these pieces always preserve their motion more or less free, which circumstance is favored by the ivory polish, which they acquire at the points of contact; for the diarthrodial cartilages, when once destroyed, are never reproduced: in short, these surfaces completely consolidate; the ligamentous parts, which remained sound, grow thicker, acquire consistence, and the disease is cured.

THIRD STAGE.

When the caries is very extensive, and the consecutive abscesses are large, and near the focus of the disease, art offers but few resources. I have seen, however, some examples of cure when the disease had arrived at this stage, and we ought, in all cases, to make use of the means recommended for the second stage: but we should not decide upon opening the abscesses or *depôts* which are the result of it, until we are convinced that we can no longer expect their resolution, and that the source of the matter which forms them is dried up, which gives us reason to believe, that the work of caries is arrested; we judge of this by the cessation of the local pain, by its absence when we cause the affected limb to be moved, by the return of nutrition, of the strength and *embonpoint* of the patient, and finally, above all, when the abscess, although it may have augmented in size, is about to open spontaneously.

If, in this stage, we are fortunate enough to arrive at the result of which I have spoken, by the repeated application of the Moxas, and the use of antiscorbutics and tonics, taken internally, which supposes a treatment of six or eight months at the least, we may then try the operation proper for these kinds of abscesses, according to the procedure which I have described in my *Campagnes*, page 399, vol. ii. and which I have re-described in the course of this work. The operation being performed in that manner, and the matter wholly evacuated, thick compresses, steeped in warm camphorated oil of chamomile, should be applied upon the exterior paries of the *depôt*, and be kept on by the aid of lightly compressive bandages. This method is, in my opinion, preferable to that which has been in use until the present time, and which consists in merely making a puncture at the top of the tumor, by the aid of a trocar, and suffering the matter contained in the abscess to drain out gradually, for, in this mode of opening, the contact of the external air quickly changes the matter, which remains in the focus of the disease, the parts are struck with a gangrenous affection, and death supervenes, a few days afterwards.

By my procedure, I succeed in diminishing the focus of infection and internal contagion, by evacuating, with the aid of dry cupping, the whole of the fluid contained in the sac; the parietes of the abscess are agglutinated together, and are more easily able to contract a mutual adhesion; in short, nature, seconded by all these means, acts, with success, against the morbific causes.

During the dressings, which must be renewed frequently, we should be attentive to maintain the parietes of the sac constantly in proximity, and to prevent the introduction of air into the wound.

As I have observed, the scrofulous femoro-coxalgia in children, presents no sensible difference in its symptoms from that which we have just described. In them, as in adults attacked with rheumatic coxalgia, luxation of the thigh can only be produced by a mechanical cause, which may be brought into action, during the course of the disease. I have likewise had occasion to treat several children, affected with this disease, and my remarks on this subject are the same as those which I have already made, in the cases of the soldiers: only, I have remarked, that the disease proceeds with more rapidity in children, and that its termination is more quickly fatal: the internal remedies of which we make use, such as antiscorbutics, joined with antiscrofulous remedies, do not even arrest its progress; whilst the Moxa, applied according to the prescribed precepts, produces wonderful effects, and constantly removes the disease, when it is not very far advanced. I might cite many examples in support of this assertion.

I may add to these reflections, that the actual cautery, so justly extolled, by the German Professor, for the rheumatic femoro-coxalgia of adults, does not appear to me to be proper in the scrofulous coxalgia of very young persons, inasmuch as the powerful and deep cauterization is attended with a destruction, in the soft parts of these individuals, so much the more extensive, from their being, both by age and disease, in a mucous state: a putrid local affection may be, therefore, quickly produced by that application. We should confine ourselves to the use of small Moxas, with the precautions which have been pointed out, and to the employment of antiscorbutics, which second, advantageously, the effects of these topical remedies.

In support of the principles laid down in this article, I shall now proceed to relate a series of cases, relative to the rheumatic femoro-coxalgia of adults, which have appeared to me to be possessed of considerable interest.

CASE 1.

Mademoiselle de St. M. aged twenty-one years, of extreme sensibility, had been troubled, for a long time, with violent pains in the left iliac region, towards the coxo-femoral articulation, as well as in the knee of the same side: these were frequently accompanied with singular neuralgiæ, the cause of which was mistaken by several physicians of Paris.

Dr. CORREF, already mentioned, called me in, at a time when this young lady was nearly dying, from the effects of a tetanic affection of the pharynx and œsophagus, the removal of which had been vainly attempted. I hastened to force the passage to the stomach, by means of a proper sound, and this was followed up by cupping *(scarifiées)*: the nervous and inflammatory symptoms had entirely disappeared on the third day.

From that time, I turned my attention to the

cause of the very various nervous symptoms, which the patient frequently experienced, and discovered, from the symptoms which indicate that period of the disease, an hereditary rheumatic femoro-coxalgia, in its second stage: there was, also, above the crural arch, and beneath the anterior spine of the ilium, a slightly prominent oval tumor, at the bottom of which, fluctuation might be evidently felt.

The inflammation, which still existed, yielded readily to cupping *(scarifiées)*: this was followed by the application of the Moxas. The first seven or eight produced an extremely favorable change: I treated the violent pains which continued to manifest themselves, by passing a seton through the thickness of the integuments, under the crest of the ilium, which was kept in, for the space of fifteen days: fresh Moxas were applied all around the articulation: after the thirteenth, the tumor had entirely disappeared.— This young lady had been affected with a purulent discharge, by the uterine passages, which was more or less abundant, according to the state of the atmosphere.

The diseased extremity, which at first was longer than the other by about four centimetres, (In. 1.574) was considerably retracted, and, although half bent, presented a diminution in length of about two centimetres (In. .787): finally, the cure was completed after the application of twenty Moxas.

Now, how can we account for the progress of nature in the fortunate and extraordinary termination of this disease? It is doubtless very difficult: but nevertheless, I think, that by applying to the subject of this case, the principles which I have hypothetically laid down, in the course of this article, we may be convinced, that there had been not only absorption of the purulent matter, accumulated in the abscess, already formed in the pelvis, behind the cotyloid cavity, but a point of caries had probably perforated it; as I have observed in an individual, who died of a similar disease, at the Military Hospital of Gros Caillou, and who probably would have recovered his health, if, like Mademoiselle de St. M. and several other patients, he had rigorously observed the regimen which was prescribed for him: but, at the moment when he gave well-founded hopes of cure, he delivered himself up to all sorts of intemperance, and even to onanism, from which he had not been able to wean himself, and died. On opening the body, we found the cartilage of the cotyloid cavity destroyed; the circumference and the bottom of this cavity eaten by the caries; whilst, on its exterior surface, a work of cicatrization, like that which we observe in the cicatrization of the soft parts, was already perceptible: the head of the femur had also lost its cartilage and its round ligament, and this apophysis was reduced by one-third of its size, from the effect of the caries, to which a true cicatrization had succeeded. The traces of a considerable abscess were also observable in the interior of the pelvis, with a thickening of the portions of the periosteum, corresponding to the focus of the disease. This pathological specimen, which I have preserved, has been presented to the Société de Médecine of the Faculty of Paris.

A similar preparation has been presented to the same Society, by Messieurs BECLARD and CLOQUET: it was found on the dissection of a man, forty years old, whose spine was affected in a like manner; these two disorders constituted in him the existence of femoro-coxalgia and rachialgia. (See the *Bulletin de la Société*, No. 7, 1816.)

But since, nature, aided by surgery, was successful, in this case, in arresting the progress of the disease, when arrived at its third stage, and in producing a cure—*à fortiori*, ought we to credit that of Mademoiselle de St. M. in whom, in truth, the disease was much less advanced, but more complicated with different symptoms, which it produced, or which accompanied it.

In this young lady, there was likewise a shortening of the limb, in consequence of the caries of the bony part of the articulation; and also internal cicatrization, and the restoration of a great part of the motions of the extremity, and of all the functions.

This person, with the exception of lameness, enjoys, at present, good health.

CASE 2.

A cavalry grenadier, aged about twenty-two years, was received at Gros Caillou, in December, 1814, presenting every symptom of femoro-coxalgia, in the right thigh, with an abscess, *par congestion*, seated at the external and anterior side of the ilio-femoral articulation of the same side. This tumor projected about three centimetres (In. 1.181), and was about five or six in length (In. 1.968, or 2.362). The diseased extremity, which could with difficulty execute very slight movements, put in parallel with that of the opposite side, passed the level, by about three centimetres (In. 1.181): every thing, moreover, announced a spontaneous luxation, if we except the characteristic signs, of which I have spoken, and which I have never met with, in any of these patients.

Several cuppings *(scarifiées)* preceded the application of the Moxas, which, until the fifth, did not give us any hope of effecting the resolution of the tumor; but, after the eighth and ninth, it was already reduced by a quarter of its size. Fresh Moxas caused a farther diminution, at which time, being obliged to leave, I confided this patient to the care of Dr. PIGOU, who, by a continuation of the same treatment, succeeded in curing him, with scarcely any deformity, or lameness, as the limb was only some millimetres* shorter than that of the opposite side.

CASE 3.

In October, 1814, I again saw a case of femoro-coxalgia, which had arrived at its second stage, in the person of M. de RONSAN (JEAN-CASIMIR), aged thirty-two years, one of the King's Body Guard. This disease was the consequence of a rheumatic affection, which wet and cold bivouacs had developed.

---

* A Millimetre is equal to In. .03937. *Tr.*

The diseased limb, longer than that of the opposite side by about four centimetres (In. 1.574), was in a state of atrophy, and almost complete immobility: there was in the gluteal region an oval tumor, in the centre of which an obscure fluctuation might be felt; other symptoms appeared to announce a spontaneous luxation of the femur, effected in such a manner, that the head of the bone seemed to rest upon one of the external points of the edge of the cotyloid cavity; but none of the pathognomonic signs of luxation were present to confirm this suspicion.

It is needless to repeat, that, guided by the motives which I have mentioned in describing femoro-coxalgia, I ordered the patient to be cupped *(scarifiées)* upon the whole circumference of the articulation. Some Moxas had already diminished the disease, when Professor Rust, passing through Paris, on his way to Berlin, advised me to apply the red hot iron upon the articular region, as a means for causing the limb to be restored immediately to its natural length; I was anxious to see and perform the operation myself, before I could credit such a result.

Three deep lines, converging at their inferior parts, were traced with the metallic cautery at the posterior region of the articulation: immediately after the cauterization, to my great surprise, the limb actually lost its preternatural length.

After fifteen days repose, the pains of the knee returned, and the extremity was again elongated by about a centimetre and a half (In. .5905), the cauterization, however, had been sufficiently deep, and had been made according to the views of the German Professor. The application of the Moxas, to which I thought it right to revert, and which I continued until the twenty-first, caused the pains and the elongation to disappear—restored the motion of the limb—and completed, in February, 1816, the perfect cure of this soldier, whose limb remained only a centimetre (In. .3937) shorter than that of the opposite side.

CASE 4.

Femoro-coxalgia is more frequently met with amongst cavalry and artillery soldiers, who, being more subjected to bivouacs, are, consequently, more exposed to rheumatic affections.

Dubois (Jacques), cannoneer, aged twenty-five years, was received into the hospital at Gros Caillou, in February, 1816. Violent permanent pains in the right knee, flexion, and difficulty in moving the leg, tumefaction around the iliofemoral articulation, emaciation, slow continued fever, the existence of an oval, deep tumor, with an obscure fluctuation at the internal side of the articulation, or at the external and posterior side, according to the attitude of the patient, sufficiently announced femoro-coxalgia.

The limb was longer than the other, by about three centimetres (In. 1.181), and when left to itself, immediately resumed its former position: at first sight, it had been affirmed that spontaneous luxation was about to be completely effected—my prognostic was, however, quite opposite. After cupping, four Moxas had calmed the pains considerably, but the swelling and elongation of the thigh were nearly the same. I then decided, as in the preceding case, upon employing the red hot iron, according to the method of Professor Rust: this application had a result equally rapid and fortunate: the diseased limb became shorter by about three centimetres (In. 1.181). A few days afterwards, however, it began to lengthen again: the Moxas, the application of which I pushed to the twenty-fifth, prevented the elongation, and succeeded in perfectly curing the limb, which remained only about a centimetre and a half (In. .5905) shorter than the other.

CASE 5.

Malo (Jean-Claude), aged twenty-three years, cuirassier in the first regiment of the Royal Guard, presented to us, in June, 1816, a femoro-coxalgia, in its second stage, proceeding from a rheumatic affection, contracted in the wet and cold bivouacs in Saxony. The symptoms, which characterized femoro-coxalgia, seemed so much to announce a real displacement of the head of the femur, from its articular cavity, and towards one of the exterior points of the edge of that cavity, that several surgeons could not be persuaded to the contrary, until they saw me employ the exploratory and curative means of Professor Rust, which was again attended with the same success. The limb lost the elongation of about three centimetres (In. 1.181), which it had before the operation. The application was preceded by cupping *(scarifiées)*, and a proper regimen. The examples which I had had, in the two preceding cases, of the tendency of the diseased limb to re-elongate, notwithstanding the cauterization, made me reasonably suspect that this phenomenon would again take place: in fact, fifteen days after the operation, it occurred; and I was obliged to apply fifteen Moxas, in order to obtain a permanent shortening.

MALO was proceeding towards a complete cure, when, after a treatment of three months duration, in consequence of a long ramble, at his first going out, he was suddenly struck with fresh inflammatory symptoms, which, in the first twenty-four hours, reproduced all the phenomena, which were remarked at the time of his entrance into the hospital. In this relapse, it is evident, that the state of chronic inflammation, of the ligaments of the diseased articulation, produced these phenomena, as the reiterated application of cupping *(scarifiées)* was sufficient to make them disappear.

The ancients have, with justice, recommended the most perfect rest in the treatment of diseases of the joints: whatever may be the apparent improvement obtained, in other respects, by the means made use of, we should not suffer patients, affected with femoro-coxalgia, to walk about, before the entire re-establishment of the functions in their primitive state of integrity, the return of the elasticity and spring in the ligaments, the cessation of the state of paralytic relaxation of the muscles which surround the articulation, and, lastly, the cicatrization of the internal ulcerations, whether they have affected the articular surfaces, or have their seat in the fibrous system; which supposes a space of five or six months at the least.

When the inflammatory symptoms resist the repeated and energetic action of cupping *(scarifiées)*, a seton should be passed through the integuments and cellular tissue of the region nearest the articulation. There are even cases, where general bloodletting is indicated—these, however, are rare; besides, the seton may supply its place: the operation for inserting it is at first accompanied with a somewhat considerable effusion of blood; this local bloodletting disgorges, successively, the vessels of the articulation;—the irritation and the suppuration which the seton afterwards produces, concur towards the resolution of the abscesses;—lastly, we confirm the cure, by the application of a fresh series of Moxas. This is what I did for MALO, after having employed antiphlogistics; and he experienced a remarkable amelioration: I nevertheless insisted upon the use of adustion, by the cotton cylinder, until the perfect cure, which took place a short time afterwards, when this soldier returned to his duty.

CASE 6.

RABOULLARD (JACQUES), aged twenty-one years, soldier in the second regiment of cuirassiers of the Royal Guard, about three years ago, was precipitated from the top of a carriage into a ditch: the wheel having been thrown upon him, he remained, during five hours, immersed in ice, and lying upon his right side: violent pains in the ilio-femoral articulation, in the knee, and lumbar region of the same side, suddenly seized him. After this accident, the right inferior extremity became about a centimetre (In. .3937) longer than the other. The pains, which were sometimes mitigated, sometimes increased, according to the circumstances in which he was placed, always, however, continued their progression.

This patient, at the time when he came to our hospital, in August, 1816, presented the signs of femoro-coxalgia: the elongation of the limb was considerable.

Cupping, methodically applied during fifteen days, took off the fulness of the vessels, and produced a revulsive effect: I afterwards traced three rays, with the actual cautery, upon the region of the coxo-femoral articulation, according to the procedure described above. Fifteen Moxas confirmed the sudden shortening which the cautery had again produced.

CASE 7.

Dunau (Abraham), soldier in the sixth

regiment of the Royal Guard, aged twenty-five years, of a lymphatico-sanguine temperament, in the month of June, 1815, after the campaign of Waterloo, began to experience deep-seated pains in the right coxo-femoral articulation, and in the knee of the same side. These pains supervened without any apparent cause, and were regarded as rheumatic: they were easier during fine weather, returned when cold and humidity were felt, and every time when the temperature suddenly varied.

Forty days stay in the hospital, during the months of September and October, palliated his disease. DUNAU believed himself cured, and resumed his duty; but in the month of January, the pains were renewed—they increased in intensity, the limb became longer than the other, and he was obliged to perform a movement of circumduction, in order to execute the act of progression. He felt, besides, the most violent pains in the haunch and right knee.

Notwithstanding the intenseness of these symptoms, it was not until the month of October that a soft tumor, with fluctuation, and without change of color in the skin, appeared upon the middle part of the sacral region.

DUNAU entered the hospital in the first days

of December, presenting the following symptoms: I remarked upon the exterior region of the pelvis, answering to the superior part of the sacrum, a tumor of the size of two fists, with fluctuation, and without change of color in the skin: it yielded to pressure, but was then felt at the superior part of the thigh, which was lengthened upon the pelvis, *(qui etoit allongée sur le bassin)* and could not be bent, without causing the patient the most violent pains: the leg was slightly bent upon the thigh, and returned suddenly to the state of flexion, when the efforts at extension were discontinued: station was impracticable.

From these symptoms, I discovered, without difficulty, an abscess *par congestion*, occasioned by a caries of the coxo-femoral articulation. Fourteen Moxas were applied successively, and I observed the pains diminish considerably after each application: after the fourteenth, the patient bent the thigh upon the pelvis, and extended the leg upon the thigh, without experiencing much pain.

The abscess was opened on the 15th of February, according to the procedure before mentioned: it gave vent to about a pint of thin, inodorous pus, mixed with albuminous flakes, and small bony fragments, the *detritus* from the caries of the head of the femur. The fifteen days, which followed this operation, passed without any accident; but, at that time, the patient procured aliments, and gave himself up to intemperance; the suppuration almost entirely stopped, and changed its nature; a serous and very fœtid matter oozed out from the wound; and an ataxic fever developed itself. These accidents were combated with success, by the means pointed out in such cases; the suppuration became of a better quality, but was only discharged in drops; the limb experienced a shortening of about a centimetre (In. .3937); the patient could bend the thigh at will, and without experiencing pain; his *embonpoint* returned each day, in a remarkable manner, and every thing gave us reason to hope for a speedy cure, which took place effectually, at the end of July, under the influence of ten or twelve other Moxas: this soldier returned to his regiment, where he resumed his duty.

I shall terminate the *exposé* of the cases relative to femoro-coxalgia, by the detail of that of M. R——, an appraiser, whom I had treated in town, for a like affection, and for which, a Moxa had been ineffectually tried, according to the method of POTT, that is to say, by introducing peas into the wound, which had been formed upon the great trochanter of the diseased side.

This fact proves still more the little efficacy of this method, as the disease had arrived at its third stage; that is to say, there was an elongation of the member, of about two centimetres (In. .7874); an abscess *par congestion* below the point cauterized; violent pain in that region, and in the whole extent of the limb; slow and continued fever, &c.

Thirty-two Moxas, applied successively, and with the precautions mentioned above, caused the absorption of the matter of the abscess, and the cicatrization of the ulcerated or carious parts—characterized by the shortening of the limb: in fine, the cure has been so perfect, that, with the exception of a slight lameness, the patient walks actually with as much facility, as before the invasion of the disease. I performed this fortunate cure, in the course of the year 1818.

I have employed the Moxa, with like success, in the lymphatic diseases of other articulations of the limbs, especially in that which is called white swelling of the knee. The effects of this caustic, which ought to be sometimes preceded by a seton passed into the cellular tissue, at the external part of the knee, may be advantageously seconded, by an uniform and graduated compression, made with linen slips, spread with pure storax, and laid carefully one upon the other:

these dressings may be left in their place for five or six days. I have remarked, in these cases, that the *detritus* of the diarthrodial cartilages, and the fluids accumulated, are absorbed; the tumefaction of the bony parts becomes gradually reduced; the ligaments acquire consistence; an ivory substance forms on the surface of the condyles, and replaces the cartilages;—in short, the cure is obtained, in process of time, and the individual preserves the movements of the joint. Finally:—This disease shall be the subject of a particular memoir, with which I shall incessantly occupy myself.

Such are the diseases for which the Moxa has appeared to me to be generally indicated, and which I have treated with the greatest success: it is easy to conceive, however, that this remedy may be useful in other chronic affections; but the care of ascertaining them, I leave to the sagacity of practitioners.

FINIS.

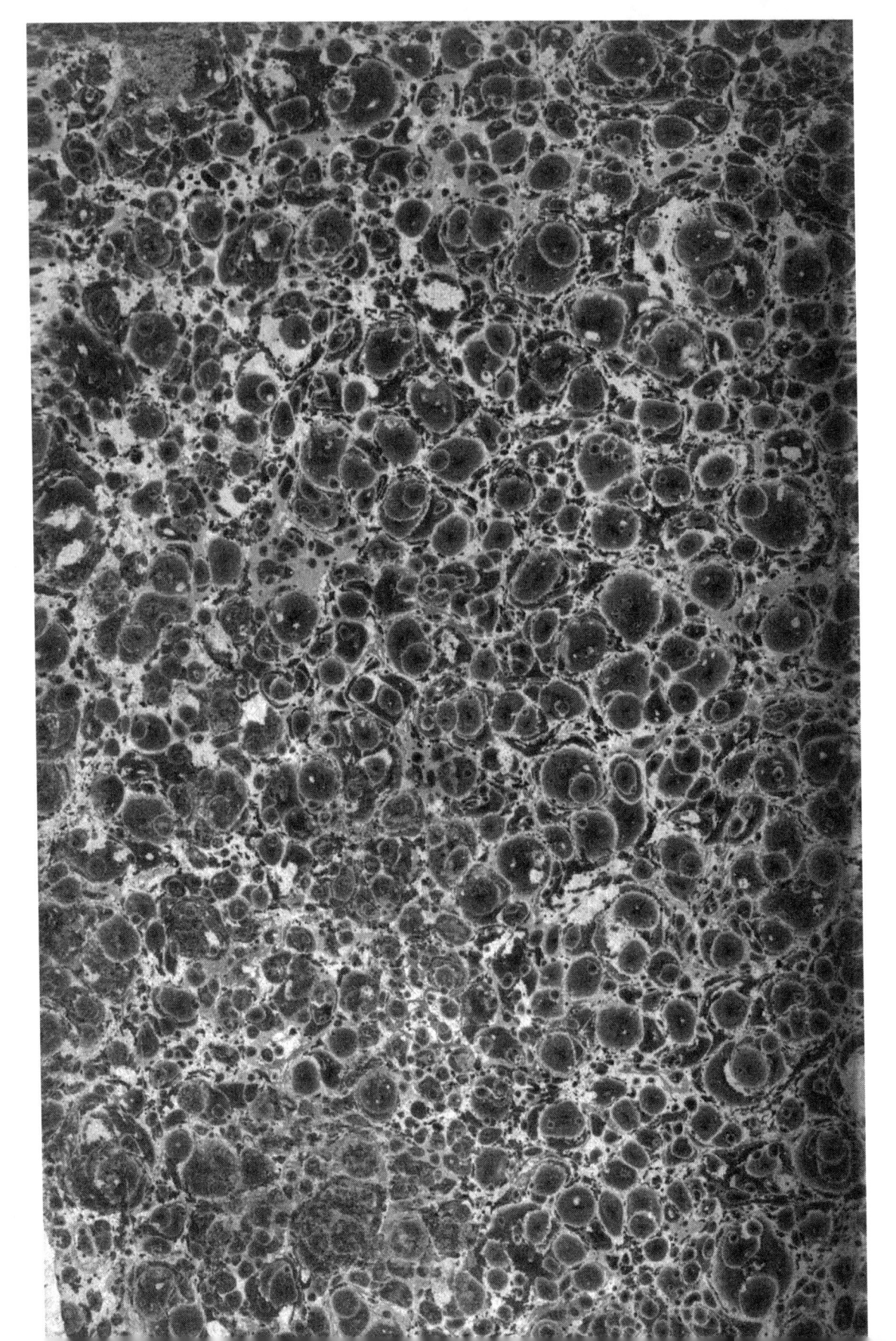